100 Churches 100 years

SED MISSO SPECULATORE
PRAECIPIT ADFERRI
CAPUT EJUS IN DISCO

VENERABLE BEDE

HISTORIA ECCLESIASTICA GENTIS ANGLORVM

ST CATHARINE of SIENA

100 Churches 100 years

Edited by Susannah Charlton,
Elain Harwood and Clare Price

BATSFORD

First published in the United Kingdom in 2019 by Batsford
1 Gower Street
London WC1E 6HD
An imprint of Pavilion Books Group

ISBN: 9781849945141

A CIP catalogue record for this book is available from the British
Library.

10 9 8 7 6 5 4 3 2 1

Reproduction by Mission Productions, Hong Kong
Printed by 1010 Printing International Ltd, China

This book can be ordered direct from the publisher at the website:
www.pavilionbooks.com or try your local bookshop.

PAGE 2 Detail from Ludwig Oppenheimer mosaic (designed by Eric Newton) at St John the Baptist, Rochdale, 1927, by Hill, Sandy & Norris.

CONTENTS

Foreword

CATHERINE CROFT

Church cases play an increasingly large part in C20 Society casework. Most church buildings, if they are still used for worship, are exempt from listed-building legislation, but have a parallel system of control overseen by church authorities. We appreciate the struggle many church communities face as congregations dwindle in many areas and expand elsewhere – both situations are problematic for the preservation of 20th-century church architecture. There is a balance to be drawn, but we are concerned when church authorities approve changes that diminish heritage value to enable different forms of worship and community use.

The quality and variety of 20th-century church architecture is worth fighting for. The significance of many churches lies in the richness and completeness of their interior fittings and decorations, making them especially vulnerable to change. Applications that C20 has advised on include complete demolition (even of listed churches), extensive reordering and dramatic sub-division. We appreciate that churches are not museums and are not maintained with public funds, yet they have potential to provide a sense of community and belonging to local people from all backgrounds and beliefs, while their beauty and the stories they tell can attract visitors to our towns and rural areas.

New academic research by authors in this volume (including the Society's own books on Stephen Dykes Bower and Maguire & Murray) is increasing our understanding of 20th-century churches and their decoration. Listing programmes such as 'Taking Stock', a survey of Roman Catholic churches, and the C20 Society's database (c20society.org.uk/c20-society-churches-database) have also broadened our knowledge. The Society runs regular tours to churches that are often otherwise locked. The Historic Chapels Trust has acquired its first 20th-century building, and we are encouraging the Churches Conservation Trust to do likewise, as well as extending its 'champing' programme to allow overnight campers to experience the changing light and atmosphere of a 20th-century church – every bit as magical as a medieval one.

This is a book to encourage everyone to visit and enjoy 20th-century churches, and to support our campaigns to preserve them.

Catherine Croft
Director, Twentieth Century Society
www. c20society.org.uk

LEFT Thanksgiving Shrine of Our Lady of Lourdes, Blackpool, 1955–57, by F.X. Verlade.

Introduction

CLARE PRICE

Looking through this volume, it very rapidly becomes apparent that any attempt to categorise British church architecture of the 20th century would be an impossible task. To begin with, phases in intensity of church building have meant that using the format of one church for each year has proved impossible. Therefore the century has been divided into blocks of years in order to give a fair spread of representative buildings across the period. Secondly, the religious architecture of the country changed beyond all recognition during the century. In response to a revolution in liturgical planning within the Christian church and changes in architectural fashion, church building evolved in both style and plan form. This was facilitated by experimentation with new materials and engineering techniques. The result is a diversity of buildings that ranges from the traditionally constructed brick basilica of St Anselm's Kennington (1914) to the hyperbolic paraboloid roof of Sam Scorer's St John Ermine in Lincoln (1963) and Richard Gilbert Scott's striking Our Lady Help of Christians, Tile Cross of 1966 (which appeared in our book *100 Buildings 100 Years*).

The first half of the 20th century in the United Kingdom is not traditionally identified with church building. However, the two books published by the Incorporated Church Building Society in 1936 and 1947 showcasing the wide range of design and prolific amount of construction that took place belie this view. Much has been obscured by later trends amongst historians to disregard the impact of religion on society and the opinions of the polemicists of the post-war liturgical movement regarding the relative unfashionability of the architecture used. New churches were needed and a large number were built, especially in the burgeoning suburbs of the major UK cities, where pressure to maintain a presence in the new centres of population forced the church authorities to react: St Thomas, Hanwell; St Alban, Golders Green; St Michael and All Angels, Wythenshawe and many others in this section of the book reflect the advance of church building into the vast residential estates built in the 1930s with few other amenities. This phenomenon can be seen across the major denominations, all of whom moved quickly lest another group gain an advantage. It was common to plant a multi-purpose building before erecting a proper church or chapel, and the latter step was often delayed and not inevitable. The architects of these churches had to contend with conflicting ideals: the need to uphold a strong tradition of church building as part of a national identity and as a fortress against change had to be balanced by pressure to reject outdated Gothic styles and embrace simplified economic designs. The hunt for an evolution of style that incorporated these ideals, while maintaining the spiritual or numinous feel of the resulting building, engaged the most prolific and famous architects of the day such as Sir Giles Gilbert Scott, Edward Maufe and Charles Nicholson. Stylistically eclectic and ostensibly conservative, the churches constructed by the Church of England in the 1920s and 1930s defy simple categorisation. The top levels of the church hierarchy were distracted by issues of Prayer Book reform and internal conflict, so concerned themselves mainly that buildings should be economical but would stand the test of time, a trend that led to traditionally constructed brick buildings with plain interiors: a *tabula rasa* to be adorned when funds allowed. These simple spaces subtly display evolutionary changes in church design, incorporating ideas from the Continent that were widely illustrated in contemporary journals and prefigured the liturgical movement that transformed the church after the Second World War. A number of churches hide their innovation under older stylistic garb which has caused their importance to go unrecognised: churches by Ninian Comper, N.F. Cachemaille-Day and J. Harold Gibbons are examples built for the Church of England. Roman Catholic church design between the wars tended to emulate the Romanesque basilican form popularised by Bentley's Westminster Cathedral of 1895. There were a very few, but

notable, exceptions to this which were the result of Continental influences. Sir Giles Gilbert Scott's Our Lady and St Alphege in Bath emphasises the importance of research into early Christianity at the time – his instructions were to produce a design that emulated Santa Maria in Cosmedin of C4–12. The centralised plans of Our Lady and the First Martyrs Bradford (Jack Langtry-Langton, 1935) and St Peter, Gorleston (by the sculptor Eric Gill from 1939) prefigured the impact that the liturgical movement would have on Roman Catholic architecture, and there were also examples of outré design such as F.X. Velarde's St Monica, Bootle, with its moderne interior. The non-conformists saw the greatest decline in church attendances of the main Christian denominations in the 20th century and this had an impact on the number and type of new church buildings that were constructed. Vast centralised halls were still being constructed by the Methodists (in Bristol, for example) but others dropped the central plan for a longitudinal chapel design in Gothic or Romanesque – again mirroring the other denominations. However, these were not universally adopted styles, especially as the 1930s progressed, as chapels such as the Sutton Baptist Chapel (Welch, Cachemaille-Day & Lander, 1934) with its cues from German expressionist architecture and the Art Deco inspired Unitarian Church of the Divine Unity, Newcastle (Cackett, Burns Dick and Mackellar, 1939–40) show. In the early post-war period, many churches maintained the pre-war single-space longitudinal plan-forms. Designs were lighter both in construction with the widespread use of steel and concrete, and in visual impact with larger areas of glass being employed. Post-war church development was stimulated by the need to replace the casualties of wartime bombing and to supply the new-town movement. Building materials were restricted until 1954, however, and it was only the Festival of Britain, which chose war-damaged Poplar in East London for its 'Live Architecture' exhibition, that enabled Cecil Handisyde to rebuild the war-damaged Congregational church there, blazing a trail for progressive modern airy churches using new materials. In their design for the new town church of St Paul's, Harlow, Humphreys and Hurst used large areas of glass to light the interior to great effect, which especially benefits the mosaic mural by John Piper – part of a post-war trend to incorporate murals into churches, often in place of east windows. American architecture was also an influence – Louis de Soissons's Unitarian church in Plymouth echoing the style of a church building that might be found in its eponymous New England counterpart. Perhaps the most influential non-conformist architect of the post-war period, Edward Mills, championed the use of modern concrete folded-plate construction, as can be seen in his Mitcham Methodist church of 1959. The centrally planned churches at Bradford and Gorleston foreshadowed a seismic shift in church planning. The Roman Catholic Church codified its elements following its Second Vatican Council in 1962–65 – the translation of the dialogue mass into vernacular languages, the celebration of all forms of mass with the priest facing the people and the concern for the proximity of the altar to the congregation. Coupled with these changes, an acceptance of modern materials and technology made new

shapes possible and completely transformed the architecture of churches. By this time, however, the Anglican Church had embarked on its own liturgical reforms, loudly proclaimed in the architectural press by an art historian-turned-priest, Peter Hammond, from 1958 onwards, and personified by St Paul, Bow Common, by Robert Maguire and Keith Murray in London's East End and completed in 1960. Respectively an architect and a designer, they edited the magazine *Churchbuilding* and in 1959 co-founded the New Churches Research Group, a multi-denominational forum that promoted a distinctively British style of new church, strongly geometric in form and with a carefully directed use of light and bright ornament. At St Paul, Bow Common, the altar is placed centrally in the square space, surrounded by the seating for the congregation. Of more lasting influence were fan shapes, as pioneered for the Roman Catholics at St Paul, Glenrothes, by Gillespie, Kidd and Coia of 1956–57 and by Sam Scorer for the Anglican church at St John Ermine, completed in 1963 and spanned by a space-age hyperbolic paraboloid roof inspired by Félix Candela. These changes in plan form were accompanied by an upsurgence of new ideas for simplified furnishings, novel artwork and stained glass. Particularly in Roman Catholic churches, where Roman Catholic émigrés provided brilliant decoration, sometimes in such unusual materials as ceramics and Perspex, jewel-like colours of abstract stained glass, mosaics and murals lift the spaces completely. Clifton Cathedral Bristol (completed by the Percy Thomas Partnership in 1973), with its fan-shaped interior and radiant *dalle de verre* glass, typifies both these trends. A central plan

and the importance of community involvement were normal concepts for the non-conformists, so the effect of liturgical form was more limited. A greater emphasis on the central acts of baptism and God's word encouraged a revival of the historic octagonal plan form, such as the Quaker meeting house by Trevor Dannatt at Blackheath, a rare example from 1972 of a powerful architectural design that survives little altered. A bigger influence was the prospect of greater ecumenism, led by a movement towards Anglican-Methodist unity in the 1960s that saw Methodist churches become more traditional with, for example, altar rails. Churches have since been transformed by a revolution in worship but also from pressures of falling attendance. Recent construction has taken the form in many cases of multi-purpose and/or multi-denominational spaces. The results are simpler spaces such as the chapels of Robinson and Fitzwilliam colleges in Cambridge. The few new parish churches to have been built have included community buildings or economic developments to provide an income. Most recently this has been distilled to an extreme form where the worship space is a small element within a larger community and residential development, such as at St Andrew, Short Street, Southwark (2006). Interestingly, in a century that would not normally be associated with religious building, six cathedrals were constructed. The two built in Liverpool symbolise not only the evolution of design from Gothic to modern but also show the change in the choices made by the church in its architects: a Roman Catholic

designed the Anglican cathedral (Sir Giles Gilbert Scott) and the Roman Catholic cathedral was designed by a non-conformist (Frederick Gibberd). These have been given a more extended treatment throughout the book to allow for the larger volume of research that is available on these significant buildings. Various important themes and influences on the religious landscape of our country have pervaded the century. These cannot be considered adequately in the short pieces on each church, so we have included essays to consider various aspects of church architecture and to highlight the most influential practices of the period. The influence of European design was something that waxed and waned during the period. Elain Harwood traces the parallel response of churches on the Continent to changing architectural fashions during the century. Increasingly Christian churches have been sharing the landscape with representations of all faiths: as synagogues, mosques and Hindu temples all form an important part of the religious journey through the century, Kate Jordan reflects on these as new landmarks. Despite times of austerity and the constant concern for economy, churches remained as important commissioners of works of art throughout the period. The desire to enrich the worship space both internally and externally encompassed a myriad of forms from murals to furnishings as discussed by Alan Powers. Artistic embellishment also formed part of the fabric of the buildings, and the change in styles and types of stained glass is covered in an essay by Jane Brocket.

LEFT Quaker Meeting House, Blackheath, London, by Trevor Dannatt, 1972.

Church Building in Western Europe 1922–75

ELAIN HARWOOD

Church building in Northern France and the Rhineland has had a bearing on Britain since before the Norman Conquest, so it was fitting that British architects should return to Europe to study the latest trends in style and construction in the 1920s. John Summerson recalled watching H. S. Goodhart-Rendel introduce Fritz Höger's work to his assistants, among them N.F. Cachemaille-Day who developed a similar love of concrete construction and expressionist brickwork. Edward Maufe published a slim guide to recent foreign churches in 1948, which highlighted the Högalidskyrkan in Stockholm of 1916–23 by Ivar Tengbom that was a source for many details in his own work.

There had been churches built in concrete and steel before the First World War, but modern church architecture truly begins in 1923 with the completion of Auguste Perret's Notre-Dame du Raincy. On the site where in 1914 General Maunoury had masterminded the repulse of the German army from the Paris outskirts, its soaring tower proclaims deliverance and peace. Perret binds Gothic construction and classical details into a single vision of naked concrete. Le Raincy begs comparison with a contemporary cradle of modernist innovation, the entries to the *Chicago Tribune* competition, yet is almost overwhelmed by Maurice Denis's sensory overload of abstract glass, realised by Marguerite Huré of the Ateliers de l'Art Sacré and an early example of the engagement of first-rate artists in French churches.

Yet perhaps the most important feature of Le Raincy is that these fireworks are restrained within a single rectangle. Perret's sloping nave follows the fall of the hill, with a sanctuary raised on ten steps within the same space. It sounds easy and again there were precedents. In Montmartre, Anatole de Baudot had built his church of St Jean in 1897–1905 as a dynamic concrete box, albeit with the altar set in an apse, and in British architecture G.F. Bodley and his pupils had reduced the chancel arch to a screen, portending the basilica churches of Sir Giles Gilbert Scott and the screens and ciboria of Ninian Comper. But Raincy strips the separation of celebrant and congregation to a concrete altar rail, reinventing the sanctuary as a stage within a theatrical space.

LEFT Notre Dame de Royan, rebuilt after Allied bombing in 1955–58. Designed by Guillaume Gillet and engineered by Bernard Laffaille (the roof is only 8cm thick) with glass by Henri Martin-Granel.

For the next forty years church architecture repeated this formula. Its legacy is tangible at Guillaume Gillet's rebuilding of Notre-Dame de Royan in 1955–58, engineered by Bernard Laffaille with a saddleback roof and 'V'-shaped wall sections to give a breathtakingly tall yet narrow, tapering section. Le Raincy also inspired churches outside France. The posh version is St Anthony, Basel, by Karl Moser from 1926–27, where the sanctuary is more defined, but more influential is its austere sibling Corpus Christi (St Fronleichnam), Aachen, a white box built without columns by Rudolf Schwarz in 1928–30. A single low aisle, separated by one marble pier that also supports the pulpit, offered a model of asymmetry continued by Schwarz after the war at St Anna, Düren, of 1951–16, where a low aisle links the long nave and small side chapel. A variant of a side chapel under a gallery appears in the work of Gillespie, Kidd & Coia, as at St Bride, East Kilbride (1957–64).

By 1960 Maufe's empirical approach was being vilified by Peter Hammond, an art student turned priest who looked to the Continent for liturgical change, seeing the structure of worship and its built form as one. The word liturgy is derived from the Greek *leiton*, meaning people, and *ergon*, meaning work, and modern church planning sought to bring together communities in shared worship. One source was the study of early Christian practices, including Gregorian chant, and the refounding of the Benedictine abbey at Solesmes in 1932 first heralded a reappraisal of the long basilicas or halls built in the first millennium. General literacy encouraged greater public participation in worship, as set out in a *motu proprio* by Pope Pius X in

1903 and extolled at a conference at Malines / Mechelen, Belgium, in 1909. The move towards a closer relationship between the celebrant and congregation was developed by scholars at the Benedictine Abbey of Maria Laach near Koblenz in Germany, and by Canon Pius Parsch in Austria. Schwarz himself was inspired by the work of Romano Guardini, whose *Vom Geist der Liturgie* was published in 1918.

As well as studying the relationship between the Eucharist and the word of God, by looking at the earliest Christian worship the Liturgical Movement also encouraged the growth of ecumenism. The Lutheran church adopted some pre-Reformation traditions such as vestments and chants, while the British Methodist church studied John Wesley's Anglican origins and reintroduced a more formal communion as part of a bid for 'Church Unity' in the 1960s. The Anglican priest A.G. Hebert brought together many of the ideas of the Benedictines and the Lutheran High Church Movement when in 1935 he published *Liturgy and Society: the Function of the Church in the Modern World*, which was followed in 1945 by Dom Gregory Dix's *The Shape of the Liturgy*.

A spiritual revival in Germany extended across Roman Catholic and Protestant denominations. Individual Protestant congregations revived the polygonal preaching box, and Otto Bartning (1883–1959) designed a church of exposed steel and glass for the 1928 International Press Exhibition in Cologne, which was rebuilt in Essen only to be destroyed by bombing in 1944. His circular Church of the Resurrection built in Essen in 1929–30 survives much restored.

ABOVE Notre Dame du Raincy, on the Paris outskirts, 1922–23. Designed by Auguste Perret with glass by Maurice Denis and Marguerite Huré; the start of modern church architecture.

By contrast, the Roman Catholic dioceses could exert their patronage across large areas, enabling Dominikus Böhm (1880–1955), Martin Weber (1890–1941) and Rudolf Schwarz (1897–1961) to specialise in designing churches. Böhm was introduced to church building by his student, Martin Weber. He designed several experimental churches in the 1920s that exploited the parabolic arch as an expressionist interpretation of Gothic architecture, with much of the structure concealed behind brick exteriors. Few were realised until in 1928–32 he built a church with a near-circular nave, St Engelbert, Cologne-Riehl, an economical means of placing as many seats as possible close to an altar and pulpit set in a shallow apse. Thence it was a logical step to

place the altar in the centre of the space where it could be still closer to the congregation, as Böhm realised in the little Christ Church, Ringenberg, in 1934–36, with the congregation on three sides round an altar placed under the crossing. While Böhm's practice centred on Cologne, Weber was based in Frankfurt, where his churches – many connected with the suburbs being developed under Ernst May – show a similar progression. His Church of the Holy Spirit, Riederwald, in 1930–31 was the first in Germany to feature a central altar, while St Albert, Dornbusch, of 1932–33, was based on a 'T'-plan. He formed a study circle for church art with Schwarz, and set out his criticisms of the separation of nave and sanctuary, and of raised altars, in an article in 1940.

ABOVE Mariendom pilgrimage church, Neviges, near Wuppertal, Germany, by Gottfried Böhm, 1964–68.

The rise of Nazism saw a hiatus in church building ahead of the wartime destruction. The archdiocese of Freiburg (serving Baden-Württemberg) reported the loss of 786 churches, while 65 Lutheran churches were destroyed in the same area. The first new churches were starkly simple, led by the emergency Lutheran church built by Bartning at Cologne-Mülheim with international aid in 1948–49, using brick and timber. He, Böhm and Schwarz combined extensive restoration work with large numbers of new churches in the suburbs flung up as the economy recovered and eight million German refugees arrived from East Germany, Poland and beyond. The archdiocese of Cologne reported in 1956 that it had built 343 churches since the war and 240 more were at the planning stage, with Archbishop Frings encouraging centralised planning. Built quickly and sometimes experimentally, the 1950s' churches tend to

be smaller and lighter than their predecessors, including steel as well as concrete, with opaque white glass and contrasts of vivid colour. The most strident feature is usually a lofty bell tower. Dominikus Böhm was joined and later succeeded in practice by his son Gottfried (1920–), whose St Albert, Saarbrücken, of 1952–53 has a single window channelling light on to the altar.

Every means was taken to bring congregations closer to the altar and pulpit, and churches took every shape from broad rectangles to 'T'-plans, clover leaves and squares, allowing seating on three sides round an altar raised on only two or three steps. Schwarz's Our Lady Queen of Heaven, Saarbrücken, of 1954 resembles an aeroplane, and other churches adopted symbolic fish-shaped plans, something also adopted by Reima and Raili Pietilä's Kaleva church in Tampere, Finland, 1964–66, as other countries and denominations caught on to liturgical thinking.

The centralised plan is well seen at St Joseph, Le Havre, where Auguste Perret set the altar under a dominating lighthouse tower; it was completed in 1956 after his death. But post-war French churches are most distinctive for their art. Basil Spence and Gerard Goalen both visited Maurice Novarina's otherwise modest Sacré-Coeur at Audincourt (1949–51) to study its glass by Fernand Léger and baptistery decoration by Jean Bazaine. This was commissioned by the Dominican priest Marie-Alain Couturier (1897–1954), himself a glass designer and co-editor of the magazine *L'Art Sacré*, and whose patronage extended to Henri Matisse for the chapel of Sainte-Marie du Rosaire de Vence (1949–51) and (with a dozen other famous names) Notre-Dame de Toute Grâce at Assy (1937–46). He also appointed Le Corbusier to design the chapel of Notre-Dame du Haut at Ronchamp (1951–55) and the convent of Sainte Marie de la Tourette at Éveux-sur-l'Arbresle near Lyon (1953–60).

Church architecture grew more diverse in the 1960s. Gottfried Böhm's churches became thoroughly mannered, their shards of board-marked concrete creating vast caverns and contrasted with art-nouveau roses in stained glass. His Mariendom pilgrimage church at Neviges of 1964–68 was followed by the Christi Auferstehung (Church of the Resurrection) in 1968–70 which combines concrete with cheap brick. Italian architects had a longer tradition of massive concrete construction, beginning at Luigi Figini and Gino Pollini's Madonna dei Poveri in Milan in 1952–54, and including Giovanni Michelucci's Madonna dell'Autostrada del Sole (San Giovanni Battista) on the outskirts of Florence in 1960–63.

Other architects chose a more quietly contemplative idiom, led in Germany by Emil Steffann (1899–1968), whose St Maria in den Benden at Düsseldorf-Wersten from 1959 led the way as a parish centre combining a church with halls and meeting rooms, often set round a courtyard. Better known in Britain are the two late Lutheran churches of Sigurd Lewerentz (1885–1975), St Mark Björkhagen, Stockholm (1956–60), and St Peter, Klippan (1963–66). These architects built in brick, with modesty yet reverence, and Lewerentz's work is exemplary of Scandinavia's more gentle modernism. A still later example is Jørn Utzon's Bagsværd Church, completed only in 1976, a symphony of pale concrete with the only colour provided by the vestments also designed by Utzon.

While it is possible to draw comparisons between British churches and contemporary European work, England's most important symbol of the Liturgical Movement, St Paul's Bow Common, looks to a different tradition. Its begetter, Father Gresham Kirkby, was disappointed when he visited the Rhineland and instead turned to an architect with a classical training; Robert Maguire's sources were the Pazzi Chapel in Florence and the teachings of Rudolf Wittkower, whose *Architectural Principles in the Age of Humanism* (1948) was also an important influence on the Smithsons' scheme for the Coventry Cathedral competition in 1951. The work of the New Churches Research Group co-founded by Maguire, Keith Murray and Peter Hammond sought an architecture without 'tricks' in contrast to the expressionist construction and decoration found in some Roman Catholic churches where refugee artists and architects from Eastern Europe played an important part.

"THOU SHALT LOVE THE LORD
THY GOD WITH ALL THY HEART,
AND WITH ALL THY SOUL, AND
WITH ALL THY STRENGTH, AND
WITH ALL THY MIND; AND THY
NEIGHBOUR AS THYSELF."
LUKE 10:27

"JESUS' THREE DAYS' WORK
IN THE SEPULCHRE SET THE
SEAL OF ETERNITY ON TIME.
HE PROVED LIFE TO BE
DEATHLESS AND LOVE T
THE MASTER OF HATE

1914-
1929

St Anselm

Architect Adshead & Ramsey
Location Kennington, London
Year started 1914
Denomination Church of England
Listing Grade II

On 14th June 1914, the Prince of Wales laid the foundation stone for a new domed
church dedicated to St Anselm overlooking Kennington Cross. Construction
was interrupted by the war and financial difficulties. To complete the building in
1933, therefore, the original architects, Adshead and Ramsey, subsumed the thick
standing walls (legacy of the proposed dome) within a cheaper design: an austere
Early Christian basilica. Sculpture by Alfred Gerrard ornaments the main door
and aisle arcades, the only stone elements in this brick building. The church was
furnished with extreme economy, with borrowed stalls, a moulded ciborium and
poured-concrete altar rail. The only notable fitting is a font by Derrick Frith of
1939. To soften the simplicity of the lime-washed interior, the artist Norman Adams
was commissioned to produce two large abstract canvasses depicting the *Pilgrim's
Progress* in 1969–71.

John Goodall

St Barnabas

Architect Ernest Shearman
Location Ealing, Greater London
Year completed 1916
Denomination Church of England
Listing Grade II

Severe, surprising and intricate, its medieval brick mass rising above the domestic
cottage scale of its garden suburb setting, St Barnabas is one of three distinctive High
Anglican, London churches designed by Ernest Charles Shearman (1859–1939), here
joined by local architect Ernest Tyler. Shearman had spent ten years with Charles
Barry Junior, before leaving for Argentina in 1889 to work on the railways. There is
a trace of functionalism in the heroic scale of the brickwork, but the true inspiration
lay in the lofty mendicant churches of medieval Italy, overlaid with a late flourish of
Gothic romanticism. Its unfinished state underscores its ambition.

Like Shearman's greatest church, St Silas, Kentish Town (1911–12), St Barnabas
is powerfully atmospheric inside. Passage aisles enhance the spatial drama; James
Clark's spirit fresco chancel paintings and a remarkable tracery-filled Lady chapel
round window are other highlights.

Roger Bowdler

Our Lady of the Assumption

Architect Giles Gilbert Scott
Location Northfleet, Kent
Year completed 1916
Denomination Roman Catholic
Listing Grade II*

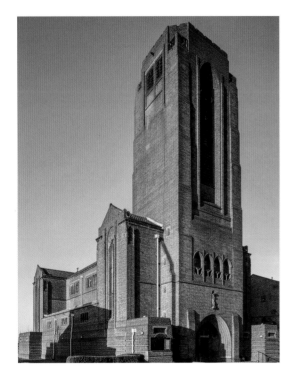

With its grooved plinth, cubic massing and tall slit windows, the Roman Catholic church at Northfleet may be the most radical church begun in Britain immediately before the First World War. The building recalls Scott's industrial designs such as Battersea Power Station, yet it predates all of his industrial work. The motives behind the design were avant-garde and formalist. Remarkably for its date, the mouldings are all abstracted into planes of brick. The tower is a prototype for the one at Liverpool Cathedral: 'It may not be a very big tower actually', critic Charles Reilly wrote, 'but it is the most powerful and dominating tower I know.' As an experiment, Scott had concrete poured into the wall cavities, resulting in terrible moisture problems and extensive rebuilding work from 2000–03. Internally, a shallow chancel continuous with the nave and removing the choir to a loft brought the congregation closer to the action of the Eucharist.

David Frazer Lewis

St Sarkis Armenian Church

Architect Arthur Davis of Mewès and Davis
Location Kensington, London
Year completed 1923
Denomination Armenian Orthodox
Listing Grade II*

The oil magnate Calouste Gulbenkian sponsored St Sarkis in memory of his parents and as a centre for London's burgeoning Armenian community, then recoiling from Turkish genocides and a brief independence following the Russian Revolution. He demanded that it follow Armenian traditions, but appointed the architect of the Ritz, where he lived. Davis copied his exterior from the thirteenth-century freestanding bell tower of St Nshan within the St Haghpat monastery complex.

Lurking amid Edwardian mansion flats, St Sarkis exudes exoticism despite Davis's use of Portland stone rather than tufa. A seven-sided belfry tops a diminutive Greek cross plan defined by cusped squinches. Inside a saucer dome soars above concrete arches, with an altar and baldacchino of marbles, lapis lazuli and metalwork by the Bromsgrove Guild and decoration by Paul Turpin. Originally seating just 51 people, Mewès and Davis added a baptistery and entrance in 1937 and a sacristy in 1950.

Elain Harwood

St Andrew

Architect Sir Herbert Baker, assisted by C.A. St Leger
Location Ilford, Greater London
Year completed 1924
Denomination Church of England
Listing Grade II

Baker felt he understood church building having been articled to his uncle, Arthur
Baker, a pupil of Gilbert Scott. He built many churches in South Africa and cathedrals
in Cape Town and Pretoria, but this is his only British parish church. St Andrew's is
lofty, dark and red; the exposed internal brickwork extends to the small, traceried
windows filled with sensitively drawn glass by Karl Parsons, who had contributed
at Cape Town. Amid the cosy clutter there stands out an entrance baptistery dome
(a precursor of the Bank of England's at Tivoli Corner) with its bronze *Peace* by Sir
Charles Wheeler and woodwork by Laurence Turner, regular associates of Baker.

The size of the church and hall complex owes much to the local builder Albert
Philip Griggs, who – abandoning Congregationalist roots – funded the north chapel
to commemorate his brother, killed in the First World War, and built the rest at cost.

Elain Harwood

Second Church of Christ Scientist

Architect Burnet & Tait
Location Kensington, London
Year completed 1926
Denomination Christian Scientist
Listing Grade II

This notable example of a non-conformist church in interwar Britain owes a
stylistic debt to Lombardic Romanesque churches yet reveals a sophisticated mix
of American and Continental influences, typical of the work of Sir John Burnet
(1857–1938) and Thomas Smith Tait (1882–1954). Commissioned by the American
socialite and politician, Nancy Astor, the brick-built church with its accompanying
Sunday school also complied with strictures set out by the Christian Science doctrine,
whereby the healing power of Bible scripture was central to the church's identity.
Christian symbols were strongly discouraged which inspired the architects to
produce an outstanding proto-modern interior scheme for the large central worship
space including high-quality bespoke furniture and fittings. Frank Lloyd Wright's
concept of an organic architecture of unifying space and materials and the geometry
of the Dutch and German modernism of Berlage and Wagner are apparent.

Dawn McDowell

St Columba

Architect Leslie Moore
Location Scarborough, North Yorkshire
Year completed 1926
Denomination Church of England
Listing Grade II*

Designed in 1914, but constructed later in 1922–26, Moore's church fills its difficult corner site exactly, incorporating additional outer aisles and polygonal chancel to produce an unusual diamond-shaped ground plan. Its angular extremities have led the plan to be described as resembling a dove – and this symbol of the church's patron is repeated throughout. It has been written that one strength of Moore's ecclesiastical buildings is their respect for context: 'from the outside they seem like massive versions of the brick terraces that surround them. But to step through the doors is to discover a quite different inner meaning' that 'increasingly reveals itself as a beautifully integrated complex of asymmetry, light and shade'. This certainly applies here – the ratio of clear to stained glass is balanced perfectly to fill the nave with bright light, while dense coloured glass is clustered in side chapels.

Sam Hawksford-White

St John the Baptist

Architect Hill, Sandy & Norris
Location Rochdale, Lancashire
Year completed 1927
Denomination Roman Catholic
Listing Grade II*

This neo-Byzantine church clad in stripy brickwork, a prominent landmark in central Rochdale, shows the influence of Bentley's Westminster Cathedral on its architect E. Bower Norris, preceding influential European essays in the style. Its structure, including the dome spanning over 20 metres, is of reinforced concrete. The Greek cross plan may owe more to site constraints and choice of precedent than liturgical intentions, but is suggestive of future developments. The outstanding feature of this building, however, is the apse mosaic, added in 1933 by Eric Newton. His original surname was Oppenheimer, and on returning from the First World War he worked in the family firm of internationally renowned mosaicists in Manchester. Here, Christ the King, the Last Judgement, John the Baptist, Noah's Ark, luscious peacocks and other themes have the vivid freshness of the sixth-century mosaics at Ravenna on which they are largely based, infused with an Art Deco modernity.

Robert Proctor

St John the Baptist

Architect Charles Nicholson
Location Lewisham, London
Year completed 1928
Denomination Church of England
Listing Grade II

No list of churches from the 20th century would be complete without one by Sir
Charles Nicholson. One of the most prolific ecclesiastical architects of the first half of
the century, he not only designed a large number of new churches but worked on many
other older churches in the country and, indeed, on cathedrals, such as Leicester.

St John the Baptist is an impressive example of his work: internally spacious and
airy but reflecting Nicholson's interpretation of 'Gothic for a new century'. This
fusion of Decorated and Perpendicular is particularly apparent in the arcade and the
window tracery. One of seven churches that Nicholson designed for the Diocese of
Southwark's great post-First World War construction campaign for the burgeoning
housing estates, although the consequent financial restrictions meant that the west
end was never completed. The church has been reordered twice, the insertion of the
corona by John Hayward dating from the 1977 works.

Clare Price

Our Lady and St Alphege

Architect Sir Giles Gilbert Scott
Location Bath, Somerset
Year completed 1929
Denomination Roman Catholic
Listing Grade II*

For St Alphege's, Dom Anselm Rutherford of Downside Abbey requested that his architect, Sir Giles Gilbert Scott, design a basilica church of the type found in early Christian Rome. The altar was thus placed in an apse under a gilded ciborium; historian Elain Harwood has identified it as one of the first forward altars in the United Kingdom. Although simple in plan, the space is only revealed gradually, with visitors entering through a porch and narthex, then crossing a side aisle to enter the nave. The walls are a celebration of Bath stone rubble, rather than a support for marble and mosaic, of which the church has none. Instead, the interior is decorated with capitals carved by William Drinkwater Gough with scenes from the life of St Alphege, an incredible cosmati pavement made from cut linoleum, and pendant lights designed as gilded sunbursts. The result is a church of exceptional simplicity and dignity.

David Frazer Lewis

1930–
1945

St Francis of Assisi

Architect J. Harold Gibbons
Location Bournemouth, Dorset
Year completed 1930
Denomination Church of England
Listing Grade II

J. Harold Gibbons (1878–1957) was a leading Anglo-Catholic church architect of the inter- and post-war period, mostly building in suburban London, but his most memorable church is probably St Francis of Assisi. This was built for High Church ceremonial and the donor of the Reckitt family of starch manufacturers insisted on Gibbons as architect despite the cost.

At St Francis an impression of light and drama is conveyed through uninterrupted vistas in an unrendered interior dominated by an unpainted ciborium (plans to gild it never being realised) and a sequence of plain rounded arches either side of the nave. It is reminiscent of his mentor Temple Moore's later churches (Gibbons worked in Moore's office from 1902–03) but more pared down, expressing modernity of form and a ghost of Art Deco.

Robert Drake

Church of the Good Shepherd

Architect Martin Travers
Location Carshalton-on-the-Hill, Greater London
Year completed 1930
Denomination Church of England
Listing Grade II

This was one of two churches in South London by the influential church furnishings designer Martin Travers (1886–1948) built with his architect partner T.F.W. Grant; the other was Holy Redeemer, Streatham. The Carshalton church was built as a bastion of High-Anglicanism with an unusual Spanish Mission west front profile (although now stripped of its white render) and neo-Baroque interior. The star-shaped light fittings have gone, but the subtly coloured and crenellated hanging crucifix and reredos above the altar and two stained-glass windows by Travers of St Nicholas and the Virgin and Child survive, as well as the barrel vault plaster ceiling. The church was built very cheaply with no proper damp course, which has caused maintenance problems ever since. Although greatly extended, the main body of the church is now looking in better shape than it has for some years and with many of Travers's fittings remaining.

Robert Drake

St Mary the Virgin

Architect John Ninian Comper
Location Wellingborough, Northamptonshire
Year completed 1931 with later fittings, consecrated 1968
Denomination Church of England
Listing Grade I

The gift of three spinster sisters, Comper's masterpiece was declared by Betjeman to 'bring the agnostic to his knees'. Comper visited Rome in 1900 and Palermo in 1905, to be enraptured by the art and planning of early Christian basilicas and explore links between classicism and medieval English work. The result was 'unity by inclusion', a vision of a continuum between Mediterranean antiquity and northern Gothic, and of English architecture uninterrupted by the Reformation.

Comper explained in 1933 that he combined English fan vaults and pendants with Greek columns and a chancel screen 'as much Italian as English', though with Greek mouldings. 'The dragons on the rood loft are borrowed from medieval Greece, while the ironwork owes most to Spain… the eastern plan of the church has its origins in France. Only to its contemporaries does the church owe nothing.' Key elements are coloured, others left like fine biscuitware porcelain.

Elain Harwood

St Nicholas

Architect Welch, Cachemaille-Day and Lander
Location Burnage, Manchester
Year completed 1932
Denomination Church of England
Listing Grade II*

The Manchester Diocese is the location of two of Cachemaille-Day's most
accomplished and important pre-war churches. His first church, in the new garden
suburb of Burnage, was a fully mature work, described by Nikolaus Pevsner as 'a
milestone in the history of modern church architecture in England'. Its modernity
is evident in its blocky forms and brick detailing, owing much to Willem Dudok
and contemporary German churches. Although the layout internally is more
traditional liturgically, employing passage aisles and a continuous nave and chancel,
the architect's skill in planning is evident in the way he handles the east end. He
protected the congregation from the noise of the trams on Kingsway with a raised
Lady chapel above vestries in the bold apse, yet also provided a broad welcoming
porch with expressionist brick detailing on the south side of the chancel, which
directs the visitor towards the base of the lateral tower and the crossing.

Michael Bullen

St Christopher

Architect Bernard A. Miller
Location Norris Green, Liverpool
Year completed 1932
Denomination Church of England
Listing Grade II*

Miller was a student of Charles Reilly at the Liverpool School of Architecture. His churches may seem solid – landmarks in suburban estates – but their interiors and detailing are often original. St Christopher's is low, Romanesque and stocky on the outside but its interior with its swooping hyperbolic vaulting and arches, glitzy eight-pointed star font, and moderne furnishing impress. The varied chancel arches appear to have a pulsing rhythm: is it a church or a cinema? The colour scheme was originally cool and stylishly jazzy but this was later repainted to Wedgwood blue: less cold-feeling. The brick exterior is linked by a cloister to the church hall. Note H. Tyson Smith's cement angel plaques. St Christopher's was the 'Children's Church', supposedly paid for with contributions from Liverpool's children: a stroke of PR genius by the Bishop.

Aidan Turner-Bishop

St Alban

Architect Sir Giles Gilbert Scott
Location Golders Green, Greater London
Year completed 1933
Denomination Church of England
Listing Grade II

The church that we see today opposite the Tube station, hunkering down next to the shopping parades of Golders Green, gives few clues to Scott's original vision for this church. Having been appointed before the First World War, this long association meant that he understood the locals' aspirations. Early design iterations show Scott experimenting with different layouts, ultimately submitting to the Diocese plans which achieved all his clients' requirements: a monumental castellated tower with landmark spire, sweeping catslide roofs leading to a human-scaled entrance door; cruciform in plan with a central altar with the choir and congregation in each arm.

Scott's modifications were made at the behest of the Honorary Advisory Committee of Architects of the Diocese: they objected to a spire 'taller than Canterbury Cathedral' and a layout they considered poor for choral singing.

Clare Price

St Faith

Architect Seely and Paget
Location Lee-on-the-Solent, Hampshire
Year completed 1933
Denomination Church of England
Listing Grade II

John Seely and Paul Paget, personal as well as professional partners, were an exceptionally well-connected couple who, in 1933, were only a year away from designing their magnificent extensions to Eltham Palace in London. St Faith's Church is a more typical example of their work, which in this case probably came their way because Seely's father was Lord Lieutenant of Hampshire at the time (he laid the foundation stone).

At St Faith's the partners decorated the exteriors of their buildings with features irregularly drawn from vernacular interpretations of late Stuart brick architecture, as they often did, but within they experimented with what became their trademark feature: a series of in-situ concrete catenary arches, well before Eric Gill used similar forms for his church in Gorleston in Norfolk.

Thus the nave has a lively, jazzy look, more precisely related to the spirit of the age than many small interwar churches.

Timothy Brittain-Catlin

St Saviour

Architect N.F. Cachemaille-Day, Welch & Lander
Location Eltham, Greater London
Year completed 1933
Denomination Church of England
Listing Grade II*

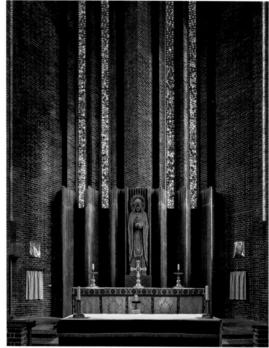

A strikingly modern example of a church built with funding from the Diocese of
Southwark's 25 Churches campaign and the first designed by Cachemaille-Day in
London. The strong fortress-like silhouette of this church betrays the architect's
German expressionist and Scandinavian influences. Jagged fins of grey-purple brick
dominate externally and internally, the motif continuing in the tower over the altar
and the pulpit, which dramatically clasps a nave pier. The tower base acts as the
chancel, illuminated by the stunning blue glass by Mellowes, deliberately short,
housing only the altar and the built-in brick clergy stalls: the choir were located in
a purpose-built west-end gallery to avoid distancing congregation from altar. The
concrete interior fittings of font, reredos and statue of Christ, which dominates
the sanctuary, are by Donald Hastings. The Lady chapel contains small abstract
windows by John Hayward added later in the 1950s.

Clare Price

Douai Abbey

Architect J. Arnold Crush
Location Woolhampton, Berkshire
Year completed 1933
Denomination Roman Catholic
Listing Grade II*

Douai Abbey church is a building of two halves: individually, each illuminates the liturgical and aesthetic culture of its era; together they tell the rich story of the Douai Benedictines. Douai has accreted slowly since its foundation in 1903 and the Abbey church bears testament to the way that piecemeal funding, drives and stalls the building programmes of religious communities. In 1928 the community chose J. Arnold Crush to design a Neo-Gothic quotation of their former church in Douai, France. Funds evaporated and building was halted in 1933 with Crush's design remaining unfinished and a temporary wall erected at the west end. By the mid-80s, the wall became unstable and the community had either to undertake major repairs or complete the unfinished design. They chose the latter and selected a bold modern design by Michael Blee, opened in 1993, which contrasts sharply with Crush's historicism and cogently articulates continuity and change in Benedictine worship.

Kate Jordan

St Thomas the Apostle

Architect Edward Maufe
Location Hanwell, Greater London
Year completed 1934
Denomination Church of England
Listing Grade II*

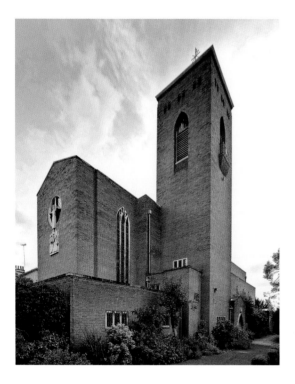

In 1932 Reverend Hubert Beck wrote asking Edward Maufe to design a church for the new residential district of Hanwell with the brief 'you know what we are out for in the suburbs nowadays'. Beck did not anticipate that the church that Maufe designed would be considered to surpass a cathedral. Indeed, St Thomas has been viewed as his testing ground for Guildford: a stunning concrete vaulted space of pointed arches, narrow passage aisles and lancet windows, a jewel box Lady chapel and children's corner as well as sculpture by Eric Gill (carved in-situ), here in the form of a crucifixion acting as the tracery of the east window. The church retains these features today, together with exceptionally beautiful fittings including glass by Moira Forsyth, textiles from Heal's and the original Ruboleum flooring patterned with the chevron motif of St Thomas. All these have contributed to the enduring charm of this church known as 'little Guildford'.

Clare Price

Sutton Baptist Church

Architect N.F. Cachemaille-Day
Location Sutton, Greater London
Year completed 1934
Denomination Baptist
Listing Grade II*

It is usual to be struck by Cachemaille-Day's debt to German expressionism when confronted with the exterior of his churches, but at Sutton Baptist Church it is the dramatic soaring arches of the interior that speak strongly of Böhm's work of the 1920s. Thought to be his only non-conformist church, as with all his work, this church is a unique expression of his consideration of the particular needs of the worshipping community. As a result, the baptistery takes pride of place, emphasised by the decorations: Christopher Webb's stained glass of part of the *Pilgrim's Progress* and Eva (known as Julian) Allen's sculptured relief framed by twisted brick columns, both adding refined but rich accents to the architecture. Externally it is plain, save for the exquisitely shaped windows – reticulated tracery dissected to its bare bones – which are similar in conception to those at his contemporaneously designed St Elisabeth Becontree.

Clare Price

Our Lady and the First Martyrs

Architect J.H. Langtry-Langton
Location Bradford, West Yorkshire
Year completed 1935
Denomination Roman Catholic
Listing Grade II

Was this the first British church designed with a central altar? Strictly speaking no, but its impact was far-reaching. Its parish priest, Fr John O'Connor, familiar with the European liturgical movement, placed the altar at the centre of an octagonal plan under a lantern, the tabernacle in a niche behind it. The church was only a chapel-of-ease, giving O'Connor freedom to experiment: the liturgical furnishings were of timber to be moved aside for use as a hall; a bar occupied the basement. The exterior is a satisfyingly primitive rusticated Byzantine. After later alterations, the architect's son, Peter, designed new furnishings and restored the altar's central position in 1974. O'Connor collaborated on books with Eric Gill, whose own church at Gorleston took a similar approach. Later, a Bishop of Leeds who knew the Bradford church well was John C. Heenan – patron of another important centralised design as Archbishop of Liverpool.

Robert Proctor

St Monica

Architect F.X. Velarde
Location Bootle, Merseyside
Year completed 1936
Denomination Roman Catholic
Listing Grade I

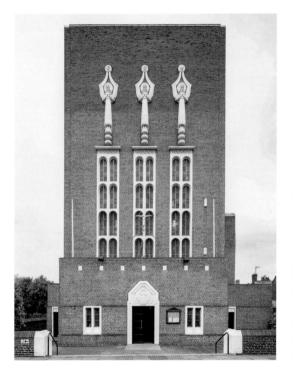

The chunky 'westwerk' actually faces east and while Velarde looked at no direct precedent, the proportion and materials reflect a German tradition revived in the 1920s. The scale resembles Otto Bartning's Pressa church, which he saw in 1928, and the arched fenestration that of Dominikus Böhm's St Joseph, Hindenburg (now Zabrze, Poland). But the incorporation of sculpture is unique, with H. Tyson Smith's angels gripping the windows like giant coat pegs.

Inside, the brown brick arcades resemble railway viaducts rather than Albi Cathedral, emphasising the stark round arch to every window. There are weighty internal buttresses yet the nave roof is flat, supported on thin steel ribs, a disturbing contrast of heavy and lightweight, shade and luminescence, old and new. How different then the reredos, suffused by concealed, impassioned light and surmounted by W.L. Stevenson's gilded angels, the one element that hints at the joyous colour of Velarde's post-war work.

Elain Harwood

John Keble

Architect D.F. Martin-Smith
Location Mill Hill, Greater London
Year completed 1936
Denomination Church of England
Listing Grade II

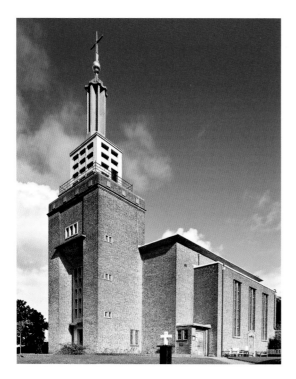 

In his 1951 treatise 'The Future of Church Building', A.B. Knapp-Fisher commended
John Keble Church as a model for new post-war churches and it subsequently became
one of the most feted of the Anglican interwar churches for its liturgical planning.
However, its revolutionary internal aisle-less shape owes much to the rules of the design
competition drawn up by the parish which, having enjoyed the choir integrated in with
the worshippers in their temporary mission church, controversially required that the
choir be located in the midst of the congregation. Martin-Smith's design was considered
by the assessor, Edward Maufe, to be the only entry that fulfilled these requirements. His
unique solution to the problem – an uninterrupted square form, with the choir in central
stalls – was facilitated by using a concrete diagrid ceiling. This, in combination with the
Swedish-influenced modern exterior, add up to make this church appear timeless.

Clare Price

St Alban

Architect Arthur W. Kenyon
Location North Harrow, Greater London
Year completed 1937
Denomination Church of England
Listing Grade II

A landmark in the local area, St Alban's tower can be seen from its approach roads and as far away as North Harrow Station. Clearly influenced by contemporary Scandinavian designs, at first sight the church appears unadorned with its plain brown brick exterior and smooth internal barrel vault. But Kenyon filled his design with detail: the unusual – almost Moorish – window heads and door framing, the finials on the pew ends (the PCC insisted on pews, overruling Kenyon's preference for chairs) and splashes of colour and decoration on the sounding boards over the ambos and in the sanctuary. Kenyon was not the obvious choice of architect: largely known for housing design, having worked with Louis de Soissons on Welwyn Garden City, he won the competition to design St Alban's as a result of the Diocesan desire to widen the field of church architects, a wistful goal of '70 architects for 70 churches'.

Clare Price

St Michael & All Angels

Architect N.F. Cachemaille-Day
Location Northenden, Greater Manchester
Year completed 1937
Denomination Church of England
Listing Grade II*

St Michael and All Angels was built to serve the incoming population of Wythenshawe, the largest council estate in Europe at the time. The design was called 'revolutionary' and 'sensational' by Pevsner. The star-shape of two interlocking squares was an evolution of an earlier multi-apsidal plan, truncated and internally re-configured following the intervention of the Bishop of Manchester. The design would have been more liturgically inventive without the Bishop's changes, with the choir in a western gallery and altar closer to the congregation under the corona (ultimately realised by Cachemaille-Day in several of his post-war commissions); even so, it was highlighted by Peter Hammond as one of only three churches of the interwar period that he considered worthy of note for its plan form. The interior is dominated by the diagrid ceiling and delicate piers which drop from it to divide the space, designed so all could see the altar.

Clare Price

St Philip

Architect John Ninian Comper
Location Cosham, Hampshire
Year completed 1937
Denomination Church of England
Listing Grade II

Sir Heath Harrison was a philanthropist from a Liverpool ship-owning family who
settled in Hampshire. His widow, Mary, offered £25,000 for a church in fast-growing
Cosham, and in 1935 recommended Comper. It was his last complete commission,
unlike St Mary, Wellingborough, built quickly and distilling Greek and Gothic sources
into a superficially simple scheme of 'unity by inclusion'.

The unassuming exterior hides an exquisite interior, four broad bays long, with
aisles and a rear choir gallery-cum-organ loft. It is light and white, with painted
glass only in the east window. For the richness is down the middle: the arcade
has Corinthian columns, the font cover is gilded, and the sanctuary is set under a
ciborium – painted and gilded, with the reservation set in one column ahead of an
intended pyx. Comper had wanted wrought-iron screens to the sanctuary; in fact the
church's very openness proved influential and suited to liturgical changes.

Elain Harwood

Our Lady Star of the Sea and St Winefride

Architect Giuseppe Rinvolucri
Location Amlwch, Anglesey
Year completed 1937
Denomination Roman Catholic
Listing Grade II*

Giuseppe Rinvolucri, a Piedmontese engineer who settled in North Wales after the First World War, designed a number of Roman Catholic churches in the mid-1930s, at Abergele, Porthmadog and Ludlow. They are historicist in style and not especially noteworthy. So why is his church at Amlwch so different, so unlikely a building to find on the north coast of Anglesey and so modern in the frank expression of its structure?

This extraordinary church consists of five parabolic segments of concrete (perhaps hinting at an upturned boat?), sitting on a masonry plinth containing a meeting room. Three of the segments are inset with crown-like strips of blue and opaque white bottle glass which give a lovely radiance to the interior. Portholes in the rendered side walls serve the meeting room. Early photographs show a more rugged appearance than the exterior has in its present, renovated condition, almost as if the concrete shells have burst forth from out of the rock.

Adam Voelcker

51

St Peter-in-Chains

Architect Gillespie, Kidd & Coia
Location Ardrossan, Scotland
Year completed 1938
Denomination Roman Catholic
Listing Grade A

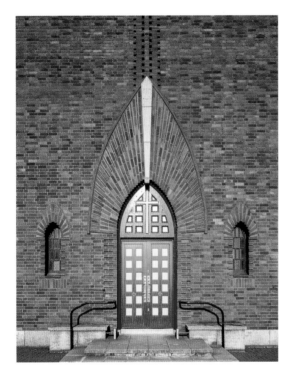 

Replacing a grand but dilapidated Regency seaside villa owned by the Roman Catholic Archdiocese of Glasgow, this church on the Ardrossan shoreline cut a striking modern and metropolitan figure in the skyline of its quiet seaside resort. T. Warnett Kennedy claimed sole authorship of the design, feasibly so since it bears little resemblance to Coia's earlier churches. It departs from Coia's Italianate inclinations to land somewhere between the Netherlands and Denmark, absorbing (no doubt from admiring perusals of Frank Yerbury's photographs) Dudok's obsessive brick detailing and horizontality and the off-centre tower of Östberg's Stockholm Town Hall. The brickwork around the entrances is brilliantly inventive, and the railings and fenestration seem to owe something to Charles Rennie Mackintosh, whose reputation was recently revived by Pevsner. The interior is a wilfully stark liturgical backdrop in cream plaster over brick piers, colour concentrated into marble furnishings.

Robert Proctor

St Luke the Physician

Architect W. Cecil Young of Taylor & Young
Location Wythenshawe, Manchester
Year completed 1939
Denomination Church of England
Listing Grade II

St Luke's, built in the cold fields of Wythenshawe for parishioners moved from
Manchester slums, was intended by Cecil Young to provide, 'a feeling of strength and
endurance' for the displaced new inhabitants of Benchill. He didn't want to strive
after 'sensational effect'. St Luke's is solid – even boxy – built in pale brick with a
chunky but subtly chamfered tower and a jolly, coloured mosaic clock. The interior
is large with a flat, compartmented ceiling. In 1984 it was reordered, creating a
community room; the reredos of Christ in Majesty was relocated. The Lady chapel
has a decorative ceilure, or panel, above the altar: concealed light bulbs in the stars.
Wythenshawe matured into a large township: the fields were built over. St Luke's
remains an enduring witness of Christian worship.

Aidan Turner-Bishop

St Mary Star of the Sea

Architect Reginald Fairlie
Location Tayport, Fife
Year completed 1939
Denomination Roman Catholic
Listing Grade B

A strikingly evocative traditionalist design by Scotland's most prominent and prolific early 20th-century Catholic architect. Resisting modernity, the traditionalist movement (strongest in the east) meant both Catholic and Protestant church designs tried to be 'national', drawing from historic precedent. Here, Fairlie demonstrates his knowledge of Scotland's historic churches: a sober simplicity evokes Scotland's pre-Reformation Catholic tradition of modest exteriors, having simple broad lancets, an apse and only one traceried window. The tower profile references the square-based octagonal tower at Elie, or even nearby Leuchars' tower, while its near-blank walling (the only ornament a Hew Lorimer sculpture of Mary and Child) seems modelled on 18th-century Caithness/Sutherland churches. The inside is also simple: a painted open timber roof (evoking Arts & Crafts antiquity) contrasts with whitewashed walls.

Diane Watters

St Peter the Apostle

Architect Eric Gill
Location Gorleston-on-Sea, Norfolk
Year completed 1938–39
Denomination Roman Catholic
Listing Grade II*

In a seaside suburb of Great Yarmouth, this was the only major building erected to designs by Eric Gill, type-designer, wood-engraver and sculptor, who had trained as an architect with W.D. Caröe. The priest, Thomas Walker, had come from Buckinghamshire, near where Gill was living, and an architect from High Wycombe was involved. The simple brick arches springing from floor level are found at Dom Paul Bellot's Quarr Abbey on the Isle of Wight (1912). The intersection at the crossing was a borrowing from French *Art Sacré* practice, for as Gill said, the church is 'first and chiefly a canopy over an altar'. Placing the altar centrally, Gill believed, would assist 'a great movement for the re-evangelisation of the people'. St Peter also displayed Gill's preferences for 'a plain building done by bricklayers and carpenters' without recourse to 'mechanical town methods'. Outline paintings by Gill's son-in-law Denis Tegetmeier appear over the crossing.

Alan Powers

Church of the Divine Unity

Architect Robert MacKellar of Cackett, Burns Dick and MacKellar
Location Ellison Place, Newcastle-upon-Tyne
Year completed 1940
Denomination Unitarian
Listing Grade II

The non-conformist congregation founded by Richard Gilpin, ejected from the established church in 1662, is one of Britain's oldest. Its social status had risen sufficiently by 1852 to commission a new church from leading local architect John Dobson adjoining the public library. But Dobson's foundations were weak and Reverend Herbert Barnes, whose inspiring sermons packed the church during his long ministry (1919–50), commissioned a replacement. His building seats 500, and there is also a substantial hall. Burns Dick and MacKellar built many civic buildings in Newcastle, and the Divine Unity resembles a public hall with its broad plan, high rear gallery and flat, coffered roof. A pulpit, reading desk and simple table dominate the small chancel. There is glass by Harry Stammers and ironwork by Wilf Dowson. The one alteration is that the choir stalls behind them have been slightly angled towards the congregation, which now averages just twelve.

Elain Harwood

Holy Cross

Architect Albert Richardson
Location Greenford, Greater London
Year completed 1941
Denomination Church of England
Listing Grade II*

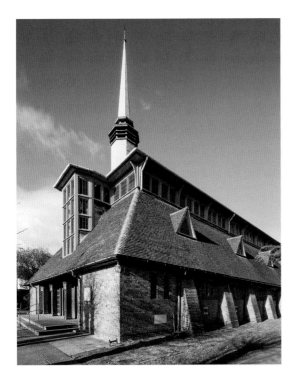

The majority of the new churches constructed by the Diocese of London between the wars were built to serve the rapidly expanding new suburban estates and therefore located on sites deliberately acquired a distance away from the existing parish church. Holy Cross is an exception to this, being located immediately adjacent to the tiny medieval church, after the original plans to replace or enlarge it were abandoned due to cost. Sir Albert Richardson designed a barn of a church for the site: not just larger then the adjacent building but of timber-framed construction, closely resembling a tithe barn with its lattice of pine beams in the interior. The exterior blends with the suburban houses more successfully than many of the contemporary designs, featuring a large square timber bay window. Despite a number of later alterations internally, the numinous feeling created by Richardson's masterly use of light still impresses.

Clare Price

1946–
1959

Trinity Congregational Church

Architect C. Handisyde and D. Rogers Stark
Location Poplar, London
Year completed 1951
Denomination Non-conformist
Listing Grade II

Cecil Handisyde designed this church (now known as the Cavalry Charismatic Baptist Church) in 1951 within the Lansbury Estate as part of the Festival of Britain 'live architecture' exhibition. He designed one of the first post-war 'church centres' with church and ancillary accommodation around a central court – a model which was to prove highly influential in new towns and estates with few community facilities. However, it is the ambitious and unusual structural design, characterized by external reinforced-concrete 'portal frames' from which the concrete roof slabs to the church and hall are hung, which are most significant. The church roof slab is also punctuated by forty domed glass rooflights, showcasing the manufacturing technology of the post-war period. Long expanses of clerestory glazing and the absence of internal structural support enhance the impression of a floating roof, and shafts of light flood through the rooflights to create wonderfully spacious, light-filled volumes.

Kelley Christ

St John the Evangelist

Architect H.S. Goodhart-Rendel
Location St Leonards-on-Sea, East Sussex
Year completed 1952
Denomination Church of England
Listing Grade II*

Blomfield did this dramatic site proud with his original brick church of 1881, the third to stand here overlooking the Channel. The nave was destroyed by a direct hit in 1943 but the tower survived and Goodhart-Rendel, well known for his interest in Victorian church architecture of all kinds, was an obvious choice to replace the losses. He created an original exercise in Gothic, with decorative banding at the wall heads and deep buttresses to the north. Internally, the lancet windows are widely framed. The blind arcade of the nave opens up to a pair of transepts before meeting the east wall with a half-arch – both being effects reminiscent of Temple Moore, whom Goodhart-Rendel admired for his originality of composition. Victorian pine was painted in 1950s pastels, and windows with designs in leading rather than colour by Jo Ledger completed the effect. The tower originally had a steeple, but the replacement was a more modest spike.

Alan Powers

English Martyrs

Architect F.X. Velarde
Location Wallasey, Wirral
Year completed 1953
Denomination Roman Catholic
Listing Grade II*

This was my favourite of my father's churches. It was commissioned before the war, which may explain its scale. My father set me to make sketch models of the exterior and the altar with its reredos; I also remember doing a visual. They were all as you would expect from a 15–16 year old, but they gave the client a rough idea.

At the opening lunch my father, always full of humour, gave a very witty speech and had the audience of prelates and priests roaring with laughter. He told me that he built in brick because he understood it; another story was that he had always wanted to build a flying buttress, novel here in an otherwise Romanesque design. He also loved gilding – at English Martyrs he used silver set against orange ceilings and bare brick walls, with sculpture by Tyson Smith, but modern chairs have overwhelmed the hallowed effect.

Giles Velarde

Dutch Church

Architect Arthur Bailey
Location Austin Friars, London
Year completed 1954
Denomination Dutch Reform Church
Listing Grade II

Tucked away in a hidden courtyard is an office block seemingly with a church attached, one of only two post-war fresh rebuilds in the City. It is a fine and harmonious composition of volumes by Bailey, who eschewed the Gothic of its significant bombed predecessor. Like a miniature cathedral with western transepts and a fleche, the Dutch Church is perched above hall and offices. The smooth Portland stone exterior is enriched by John Skeaping's relief sculptures above the paired oblong lights of the principal space.

Entry via a staircase in the north transept leads to a short aisle and the lofty nave. The minister's central desk presides over the space, its panelled timber back and tester reaching towards the coved barrel vault. The concrete box frame is hidden behind Doulting stone. Internal austerity is relieved by delicate fluted pilasters, Max Nauta's jewel-like west window and Hans van Norden's eye-catching tapestry.

Diana Coulter

Colinton Mains

Architect Ian Lindsay & Partners
Location Oxgangs Road, Edinburgh
Year completed 1954
Denomination Church of Scotland
Listing Category B

This landmark church, located on a large post-war housing estate in south west Edinburgh, is a master class in the use of vernacular idioms in a modern building. The external harling, smooth and bright, presents a traditional feel on approach, this finish and the prominent square tower influenced by the historic churches of Caithness. The interior clearly displays the evidence of Lindsay's commissions renovating churches such as Canongate Kirk in the city, which the pulpit clearly references. Surprisingly spacious, the interior is a single, plainly decorated space which was originally deliberately furnished with a mixture of pews and chairs for flexibility, allowing for smaller gatherings around the altar, before re-ordering in the early 21st century. Extra seating is incorporated in a raked western gallery and the choir located in a northern gallery. In 1965 the complex was completed with the addition of complementary halls by the same architects.

Clare Price

Notre Dame de France

Architect Hector Corfiato
Location Westminster, London
Year completed 1955
Denomination Roman Catholic (French church)
Listing Grade II

A church for London's French community was built in 1865 by Louis-Auguste
Boileau on the site of Robert Barker's circular Panorama of 1793. It was restored
after war-damage, but in 1953–55 was replaced with a new church that followed
the Panorama's footprint. Another condition was that classical columns should be
introduced, but although the Greek-born, French-trained Corfiato was a classicist he
sought to impart as modern a touch as the church would permit. The brick exterior
combines reticence with a welcoming portal.

   The result is an amalgam of progressive and conservative trends. It is a showcase
for *L'Art Sacré* – notably the chapel painted by Jean Cocteau in a week in November
1959, but also Dom Robert de Chaunac's Aubusson tapestry of 1954 and mosaics
by Boris Anrep. The sanctuary had twin pulpits, removed in a reordering by Gerald
Murphy despite the listing.

Alan Powers

St Columba

Architect Edward Maufe
Location Chelsea, London
Year completed 1955
Denomination Church of Scotland
Listing Grade II

This was Maufe's major post-war church commission, replacing a church destroyed by enemy action. Maufe was not a Scot but immersed himself in its building traditions once appointed in 1943. It reflected his ideas of incorporating social spaces below the church which he had pioneered in the 1920s in his churches for the deaf in Acton and Clapham.

Maufe's inspiration for the design stems from Sweden but the tower recalls Scottish crown steeples. The church interior reflects Presbyterian austerity and impresses with its scale, through the use of a reinforced-concrete frame allowing a 12-metre nave span, and its carefully chosen sculpture by Vernon Hill and stained glass by Moira Forsyth. The most arresting feature is the heraldic, coloured plaques representing the 33 historic counties of Scotland.

This is a striking church on a prominent but constrained site, demonstrating inside and out Maufe's mastery of spatial planning.

Robert Drake

St John the Evangelist

Architect S.E. Dykes Bower
Location Newbury, Berkshire
Year completed 1957
Denomination Church of England
Listing Grade II

The bombing of Butterfield's 1860 church in 1943 led to a sensational replacement by Dykes Bower, drawing on the brickmaking tradition of the district and recalling Butterfield's patterned polychromy with sensitive exuberance. The repetition of round-arched windows on the tall nave is suggestive of ancient Rome, as are the massive forms of the tower with its blind arcading and chunky buttresses. Dykes Bower built only three new churches, and never rated them as highly as his work in existing buildings, but St. John's, the most fully realised and largest of the set, is an astonishing achievement, not least in its balance of decoration and control, outside and in, where the painted ceiling recalls Victorian restorations such as Edward Poynter's work for Burges's restoration of Waltham Abbey. In the 21st century, when pattern and ornament have finally been unleashed again, there is much to learn from it.

Alan Powers

Our Lady of Lourdes

Architect F.X. Velarde
Location Blackpool, Lancashire
Year completed 1957
Denomination Roman Catholic
Listing Grade II*

In the forest of 'isms' that has sprouted up in architecture and design, I cannot find one in which to fit my father's work. The memorial chapel, while untypically a stone building, is like many of his other churches in carrying external decorative sculpture, here by local sculptor David John. It was conceived by Thomas E. Flynn, Bishop of Lancaster, as a memorial to the diocese's deliverance from the Second World War, for which the community raised £50,000.

The concentration of so many of Velarde's favourite motifs has created a jewel box. Here are gold mosaic columns, abstract glass in pink and blue, and a faceted ceiling painted blue in the nave and red in the sanctuary. The altar is also by John.

Listing (within 48 hours) saved the shrine from demolition, and it has been vested in the Historic Chapels Trust, but recent building work has caused further damage.

Giles Velarde

St Oswald

Architect Sir Basil Spence
Location Tile Hill, Coventry
Year completed 1957
Denomination Church of England
Listing Grade II

The Bishop of Coventry commissioned three churches for Coventry's suburban housing at Tile Hill, Willenhall and Bell Green, for which Spence promised a 'simple, direct, topical and traditional solution'. Costs were reduced by using the same construction firm and material as those employed for nearby housing. Funding came from the War Damage Commission in compensation for one destroyed inner-city church.

Their basilican form is derived from that of Coventry Cathedral (then under construction), with a concrete portal frame giving dignity and rhythm to the rugged interior. Like its sister churches, St. Oswald has extensive glazing, a patterned ceiling, lettering by Ralph Beyer, and robust chancel furniture. An appliqué hanging was made by Gerald Holtom for the altar wall and a beaten copper sculpture by Carroll Simms for the east gable. A low-slung hall at right angles (rebuilt in 2000) and openwork concrete tower define the boundary of a garden enclosure.

Louise Campbell

Baptist & Unitarian Church

Architect Richard Fraser of Louis de Soissons Partnership
Location Plymouth, Devon
Year completed 1958
Denomination Unitarian/Baptist
Listing Both listed Grade II

Plymouth's two oldest dissenting congregations lost their churches in the Blitz of 20–21 March 1941. Both were offered new sites in Patrick Abercrombie's master plan but it was only in 1957 that the land and money was secured to build two churches at right-angles to each other. The neo-Georgian style by a local architect suggests the churches built by the Pilgrim Fathers' descendants in New England. The Baptists' complex includes a hall and schoolroom linked by an arcade to the church, its spire completed only in 1959. Bracketed pediments were inspired by Inigo Jones's St Paul's Church, Covent Garden.

Both churches have little-altered interiors dominated by large murals, that in the Unitarian Church by local artist Jack Pickup, that for the Baptists painted by the leading church muralist Hans Feibusch in 1960. It is rare to find such fine and complete post-war non-conformist churches, rarer still to find two together.

Elain Harwood

Mary Harris Memorial Chapel

Architect E. Vincent Harris
Location Exeter University, Devon
Year completed 1958
Denomination Church of England
Listing Grade II

I pity Vincent Harris, a Devon man, given the dream job in 1931 of building his county's first university, only to be dismissed in 1953 in favour of the (briefly) fashionable planner, William Holford. Yet, admirably, he remained committed to building a chapel in his mother's memory, at his own expense, though from being at the centre of a formal campus its site was sidelined in Holford's revised, more sinuous plan.

Harris softened his original neo-Georgian proposals, first exhibited in 1943, by introducing two pairs of full-height Elizabethan bay windows similar to those on his nearby science buildings. They complement the solid-oak pews set in collegiate fashion in the whitewashed, softly lit interior. The one modern element and note of colour is the muted mural of abstract geometries of 1956 by Thomas Monnington, who had recently painted a similar ceiling in situ for Harris at Bristol Council House.

Elain Harwood

Church of the Ascension

Architect Robert Potter of Potter & Hare
Location Crownhill, Plymouth
Year completed 1958
Denomination Church of England
Listing Grade II

Potter was deeply interested in new developments in Christian worship and had worked with W.H. Randoll Blacking, a pupil of Ninian Comper. At the Church of the Ascension, Potter continued Comper's 'unity of inclusion' through mixing seemingly disparate stylistic elements and materials into a gloriously unified whole.

There is much to delight and intrigue: the interior given the joy of colour with the vaulted concrete ceiling painted a rich dark maroon; the horizontal emphasis of the panes to the leaded clear glazing with subtle tints filtering the outside view of trees; the exquisite detailing of the limed-oak staircase to the western choir and organ gallery; the elegant bell-shaped polished stone font bordered by an indoor geranium garden; the bold sculptural leading to Geoffrey Clarke's jewel-like hexagonal east windows. However the abiding feature that dominates the light-filled interior is the gilded ciborium, with seating around three sides, bringing the Eucharist to the heart of the church.

Robert Williams

Finnish Church

Architect Yorke, Rosenberg and Mardall
Location Rotherhithe, London
Year completed 1958
Denomination Lutheran
Listing Grade II

From the street, the Finnish Church could be a modest 1950s office block clad in Portland stone. Only the detached concrete bell tower gives it away. Originally built as a 'home from home' for Finnish seaman working in the nearby docks, it still acts as a magnet for the Scandinavian diaspora. It houses a shop selling Finnish products to homesick expats, a hostel, terrace and meeting rooms available to rent. In truly Nordic style, it even has its own sauna.

The church itself is a beautiful double-height space – flooded with natural light, lined with timber and slate. Thanks to the forethought of the architects, it is a truly versatile space – regularly hosting all kinds of activities from yoga to Christmas markets, with a mini-library in the first-floor gallery. The giant folding double doors at the back of the nave give onto a cafeteria – meaning services end with the aroma of coffee and cinnamon rolls.

Henrietta Billings

St Paul

Architect Gillespie, Kidd & Coia
Location Glenrothes, Fife
Year completed 1958
Denomination Roman Catholic
Listing Category A

The acclaim St Paul's received on its completion was inversely proportional to its modest size and budget. It was the simplicity and directness of job architect Andy MacMillan's design that attracted praise, with an 'effective use of simple materials in their natural form', as a critic at the *Architect & Building News* put it. The blank white-painted brick walls suggest more Scandinavian than Scottish influences, and give a stark background to emphasise the liturgical ceremonies. Pine boarding, coloured glass in a thick timber framework and ivy creeping up the sanctuary wall lend warmth to the interior. The wide wedge-shaped plan brings the congregation into intimate proximity to the altar. Benno Schotz made a sculpture of the Virgin and Child and a celebrated modern metal crucifix with symbols of the Passion. This church demonstrated how the modern movement could eschew cathedral-like ambitions to meet parish needs with thoughtful economy.

Robert Proctor

Methodist Church

Architect Edward Mills
Location Mitcham, Greater London
Year completed 1959
Denomination Methodist
Listing Grade II

Edward Mills's zeal for practical modern buildings was only matched by his strong
yet generous Methodism. He was equally at home designing innovative concrete-
framed factories and simple churches, and the two elements came together in his
masterpiece, on a prominent site overlooking Mitcham Common, replacing two
war-damaged churches nearby. The folded slab zig-zag roof engineered by Ove
Arup & Partners denotes the church itself and shields a cloister. It distinguishes the
church from the much larger complex of hall and classrooms alongside, for Mills
was the leading champion of the church as community centre. The modest yet
dignified interior is brightly lit from high windows to either side, with a fully glazed
bay casting light across the sanctuary. However, the roof is lined in timber and the
sanctuary wall clad in York stone, giving an unexpected touch of warmth rather like
the man himself. Mills also designed the fittings.

Elain Harwood

St Michael's College Chapel

Architect George Gaze Pace
Location Llandaff, Cardiff
Year completed 1959
Denomination Church in Wales
Listing Grade II*

After asking for a building fitting others around the quad, the college's committee criticised this stone-built chapel as 'no more than a barn', unaware that it was probably inspired by Rudolf Schwarz's St Albert, Leversbach (1932–33). Both architects believed in 'atmosphere' as a primary function of churches. Pace drew on vernacular architecture to create the effect of sunbeams cast through barn ventilation slots, using concrete-framed windows.

Pace claimed this modest chapel as an exemplar for modern church design: 'probably the most completely integrated church building erected in this country during the last 30 years' and comparable with those in Germany and Scandinavia. He believed church buildings should be 'integrated wholes', and used the same team of trusted craftsmen, mainly Yorkshire-based, wherever he worked: the hands to his head. Even the pews here were transported from Sheffield.

Judi Loach

St Paul

Architect Sir Basil Spence
Location Sheffield, South Yorkshire
Year completed 1959
Denomination Church of England
Listing Grade II*

The rapid and economical construction of the three Coventry churches brought
Spence two commissions in suburban Sheffield.

As at Coventry, everyday materials were dignified by careful proportions,
judiciously commissioned artworks and attention to site and planting. The influence
of Scandinavian architecture is evident in the warm brickwork and timber, and in the
simplicity of the design. The church is glazed at each end, with cranked brick walls
and a clerestory, above which the lightweight lattice-work roof appears to float.
Its symbolism is conveyed in the progression from font to altar and to the world
beyond, glimpses of which serve as a trigger for prayer and contemplation. Attention
is directed to the altar by the frontal designed by Anthony Blee and embroidered by
Beryl Dean in lurex, gold and silver wire, and a wrought-iron altar set donated by
Spence. A brick bell-tower is linked to the church by a covered way.

Louise Campbell

St Paul

Architect Humphreys and Hurst
Location Harlow, Essex
Year completed 1959
Denomination Church of England
Listing Grade II

St Paul's is best approached on a sunny afternoon from the west. The golden stock brickwork and copper flèche contrast with the third-rate retail developments rearing up behind: a sacred gem surrounded by profanity.

Enter, and the light flooding the interior, both through the expanse of concrete tracery and miniature slivers of stained glass at the lower levels, elevates the senses. Primary colours adorn the soffits and furnishings. This thoroughly conceived interior perfectly frames a John Piper mosaic, depicting Christ in the house of Emmaus and is contemporaneous with his more abstract composition at BBC Television Centre.

Designed by Derrick Humphreys, St Paul is assured in both the whole and in its detail, with Reginald Hurst responsible for the fittings and pews – which are remarkably intact. They worked for N.F. Cachemaille-Day (and latterly with J Harold Gibbons), before designing churches for the Diocese of Chelmsford, of which this is their masterpiece.

Des Hill

St Andrew

Architect Basil Spence and Partners
Location Clermiston, Edinburgh
Year completed 1958
Denomination Church of Scotland
Listing Category A

St Andrew's is Spence's only completed parish church in Scotland. On an Edinburgh hilltop site, its simple west end is gabled and white-harled. To one side is the bell tower; to the other the hall, with a sloping roofline to enhance the perspectival effect. The church itself is essentially rectangular in plan. Typically for Spence, careful attention was given to lighting, both natural and electric. There is a seven-by-three grid of square windows on each of the long, white-plastered walls; taller windows illuminate the sanctuary. The end wall is of exposed rubble, bowed to make a subtle V-shape with *cissus antarctica* plants trained to grow up it. Scandinavian influences are evident in the timber-clad ceiling, light fixtures, and the original Danish chairs.

St Andrew's recalls Spence's contemporaneous churches in Coventry, but it is less monumental. It embodies the fusion of tradition and modernity that is at the heart of Spence's best work.

Alistair Fair

1960–
1969

The Most Holy Trinity

Architect H.S. Goodhart-Rendel
Location Dockhead, London
Year completed 1960
Denomination Roman Catholic
Listing Grade II*

'This is the last of the big ones' the Cardinal is reported to have said at the consecration of Dockhead, the replacement for a bombed church of 1834 and its Pugin convent. Goodhart-Rendel had died by this time, with new work still in progress, including the comparable Our Lady of the Rosary in Old Marylebone Road. At Dockhead, the design, based in plan and elevation on equilateral triangles appropriate to the dedication, is delightfully intricate but not fussy. The exterior, set among tenements and dock warehouses, uses polychromy more sensitively than Butterfield, involving complex bonding patterns, such as the guilloché over the west window, simply for fun. Inside, the mood is cool and the cleverness more concealed, playing on Romanesque vaulting patterns, with a bright ceramic reredos by Cecil Atri Brown. The engineer was Felix Samuely and Partners, and rustproof 'Delta Metal' was used to reinforce the concrete vaults, lest rust corrupt such treasures on earth.

Alan Powers

St Andrew & St George

Architect Seely and Paget
Location Stevenage, Hertfordshire
Year completed 1960
Denomination Church of England
Listing Grade II

By the late 1950s John Seely was surveyor to the fabric of St Paul's Cathedral and, with Paget, was much engaged in restoring and building new churches in the diocese. St George's (its dedication until 1984) is the most prominent and successful of these. The exigencies of post-war building had a bracing effect on the concrete-framed, catenary-arch formula that the architects had been developing since the 1930s, and here the entire building imparts a feeling of being within a living, breathing skeletal form, appropriate for a major public building on a prime site in the organically designed new town of Stevenage. The muscle-like interlaced arches of the nave have a delicacy that the partnership never achieved elsewhere.

Perhaps because of this anthropomorphic feeling, the interior is uncharacteristically warm in character for a post-war church. The east window was designed by Brian Thomas, who often collaborated with the architects.

Timothy Brittain-Catlin

Our Lady of Fatima

Architect Gerard Goalen
Location Harlow, Essex
Year completed 1960
Denomination Roman Catholic
Listing Grade II

Gerard Goalen was one of the most significant architects of Roman Catholicism in the post-war period, responsible for designing dignified and noble churches that embody liturgical reform ideas. His church at Harlow is a classic statement of mid-century aesthetics. It has a spare reinforced concrete frame, 'expressed' following the Continental work of Auguste Perret and Rudolf Schwarz, and allowing great expanses of stained glass (by Charles Norris) and plain brickwork. It is more conservative in appearance than contemporary Continental work, the low-pitched, exposed concrete roof beams and purlins rather utilitarian, and at odds with the decidedly ecclesiastical wall treatment. Nonetheless, its T-shaped plan is a clear and straightforward expression of liturgical reform principles that sought to put the Mass centre-stage, enveloped by the congregation. And what a stage! The sanctuary looms large within the church, its apron a perfect square close to all congregants, and visible to all.

Gerald Adler

St Paul

Architect Robert Maguire and Keith Murray
Location Bow Common, London
Year completed 1960
Denomination Church of England
Listing Grade II

The church at Bow Common is the greatest early achievement of the liturgical Movement this side of the Channel. Its genesis was a plan Bob Maguire had drawn while still a student at the Architectural Association, a homage to Mies van der Rohe with its cranked brick wall enclosing an off-centre altar. As executed, the design embeds the altar, *matryoshka*-fashion, within concentric rectangles of raised brick pavements, with a colonnade defining an ambulatory. At its heart is a ciborium over the altar table, formed of welded, standard steel sections, 'centred' by a hanging corona above. Keith Murray brought his passion for the Eastern Orthodox to bear, with his design for the mosaics (realised by Charles Lutyens) around the spandrel panels beneath the brick box supporting the glass lantern above the sanctuary. The church thus brings the artist-craftsman's hand to an otherwise brutalist concept. Ian Nairn wrote: 'It is completely fresh, the perennial force seen again for the first time'.

Gerald Adler

St Leonard

Architect Giles and Adrian Gilbert Scott
Location St Leonards-on-Sea, East Sussex
Year completed 1961
Denomination Church of England
Listing Grade II

In 1831, James Burton placed a Gothic chapel against a chalk cliff as the centrepiece of his model resort, named St Leonard's after a lost medieval settlement. Destroyed in the war, the importance of the church's rebuilding led to this rare collaboration by the Scott brothers, a consummation of their designs for Coventry Cathedral and SS Mary and Joseph, Lansbury, which had been the first in a series featuring sensuous concrete parabolic arches and Hornton stone dadoes. Adrian Scott thought that 'no architect could wish for a more romantic or inspiring site on which to build a church', though the cliff has proved unstable and is shored up from within the church. The pulpit is the prow of a fishing boat imported from Galilee by the long-serving rector, Canon Griffiths, who also commissioned the stunning Reyntiens glass. The lectern is a ship's binnacle and exquisite fish motifs are cut into the chancel floor. The building closed in July 2018 and is threatened with demolition.

Clare Price

St Columba

Architect Wheeler & Sproson (restored, Gray Marshall Associates, 2004–08)
Location Glenrothes, Fife
Year completed 1961
Denomination Church of Scotland
Listing Category A

St Columba is a prestigious town-centre church, yet was designed both economically and experimentally, with a freestanding steel tower. The young firm challenged the Church of Scotland's risk-averse policy of building modest dual-use hall-churches, and the theologian Professor James Whyte (who was linked to the New Churches Research Group) helped to produce a truly modern church based on liturgical and social needs.

The plan and profile reverted to post-Reformation principles, specifically Scotland's outstanding centrally planned kirk: the nearby Burntisland Parish Church of 1592. The lightness of St Columba contrasts with Burntisland's solidity. Square in plan, a raised central area accommodating the pulpit and communion table is set beneath a lightweight square cupola with coloured glass and a copper roof. The mural is by Alberto Morrocco.

Diane Watters

Scargill Chapel

Architect George G. Pace
Location Kettlewell, North Yorkshire
Year completed 1961
Denomination Inter-denominational
Listing Grade II*

The setting is stunning. Pace's limestone chapel sings out over the valley, its shingled cruck roof steeper than those of the characteristic field barns yet perfectly attuned. Inside, a staircase winds up from inferior accretions with just enough drama to make the simple rectangle of the denouement chapel a surprise. Clear glazing allows glimpses of the hills, Pace's pews line three sides and a broad yet austere sanctuary projects from the long fourth.

A forward altar was novel in 1960 but befitted a progressive group of Anglican evangelists from Lancashire. In 1957 Reverend Bernard Jacob led a mission to Dales' villages, where dreams of opening a centre for family holidays and gospel studies took shape on finding the Victorian Scargill House for sale. Pace was appointed architect once the purchase was secured and the centre opened in 1959, but the chapel was realised only thanks to an anonymous donation.

Elain Harwood

COVENTRY CATHEDRAL

Architect Sir Basil Spence
Location Coventry
Year completed 1962
Denomination Church of England
Listing Grade I

Coventry Cathedral was built between 1954 and 1962, adjoining the medieval guild church of St Michael, which was raised to cathedral status in 1918 and gutted during a German air raid in 1940. An architectural competition in 1950–51 was won by Basil Spence with a design which incorporated the ruined nave and tower, placing the new cathedral at right angles, connected by a columned porch. The external walls were of reddish sandstone similar to those of its medieval predecessor, and the entrance was fully glazed to permit views inward from the city and views outward to the ruins.

The new cathedral was conventionally planned, with an altar set in a sanctuary at the head of a long nave, separated by stalls for choir and clergy. Spence suggested a more progressive arrangement for the 'east' end in 1952 but it was rejected. However the cathedral included two centrally

planned chapels, the innovatory Chapel of Unity, representing the unity of all Christian churches, and the industrial chapel.

Spence described the cathedral as three buildings in one, corresponding to different phases of the project and his evolving style. The first, spanning the period between the competition and the start of building work, had a robust, ground-hugging character. That of the second, dating from 1956 and a serious financial crisis, was austerely simple, with masonry pared back where possible in favour of concrete. The third phase, dating from the early 1960s, was bolder and more sculptural.

The un-windowed north (liturgical 'east') end with its angle buttresses presents a quasi-fortified appearance. The zig-zag side walls with narrow window apertures function as integral buttresses to carry the weight of the roof. The enormous, convex baptistery window (braced by a hidden tie rib) contains a grid of sturdy mullions and transoms. A sparer approach is evident in the cylindrical flanking chapels, built in concrete and faced in slate, and in the cathedral interior, faced in roughcast concrete blocks, where two rows of tapered concrete columns support a decorative ceiling canopy. The spacing of these columns and the design of the canopy echo those of the medieval cathedral. The porch, covered with a boxy tripartite vault, was the last and grandest element of the design, crowning the approach steps and complementing the powerful bronze figure of St Michael vanquishing the devil beside it.

Spence commissioned artworks for the interior – tapestry, stained and engraved glass, carvings for the nave recesses, a monumental altar cross and candleholders – from the leading artists of the period, many of whom had worked at the Festival of Britain. Dominating the interior is Graham Sutherland's Christ in Glory in the Tetramorph, reminding visitors of the Christian doctrine of sacrifice and resurrection which permeated the iconography of the cathedral, most notably in the device of connecting the ruins of the old cathedral to the fabric of the new one.

Criticised in the 1960s for its liturgical inflexibility, the cathedral is now recognised as an eloquent document of its time, a memorial to the victims of the Coventry Blitz and a monument of the nation's post-war reconstruction.

Louise Campbell

ABOVE Coventry Cathedral interior, looking towards Graham Sutherland's tapestry behind the sanctuary.

St Bride

Architect Gillespie, Kidd & Coia
Location East Kilbride, Lanarkshire
Year completed 1963
Denomination Roman Catholic
Listing Category A

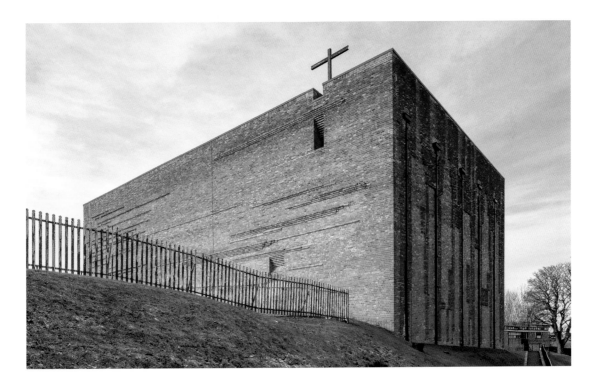

St Bride's was designed by Andy MacMillan and Isi Metzstein in 1958 largely as built, a bold and complex essay in brick brutalism applied to church architecture. Granted a prominent site at the heart of the new town, Bishop James Donald Scanlan of Motherwell demanded 'a church of the architectural distinction appropriate to this great venture in town-planning'. The young architects designed a tall brick box with deep walls, cut through for doors and light scoops, its surfaces etched with playful random brick patterning, and roofed with industrial skylights, concealed inside with timber slats. A campanile of brick slabs once balanced this volume at the edge of a piazza-like forecourt, but was demolished in 1983. A concrete gallery formed a low, dark threshold. This church was internationally published after completion with arresting photographs emphasising its dramatic sculptural forms, and its influence is evident in many other churches of the sixties.

Robert Proctor

St John the Baptist

Architect Sam Scorer
Location Lincoln, Lincolnshire
Year completed 1963
Denomination Church of England
Listing Grade II*

The parish church of St John the Baptist is located on Lincoln's residential Ermine Estate. It was consecrated in 1963.

Designed by the architect Sam Scorer in consultation with structural engineer Dr Kálmán Hajnal-Kónyi, this 'church of tomorrow' is both architecturally bold and theologically cogent. It is a concrete and glass structure topped by an inverse hyperbolic paraboloid roof. The simplicity of the exterior belies the aesthetic and spiritual drama within. A massive concrete font occupies the centre of the church, its lowest point: a pilgrim-visitor descends into the symbolic waters of baptism before ascending the sanctuary steps to the altar of salvation. Above, Keith New's dominant, transcendent east window depicts *The Revelation of God's Plan for Man's Redemption* in vibrant colour and form.

Ben Stoker

Church of the Good Shepherd

Architect Gerard Goalen
Location Woodthorpe, Nottingham
Year completed 1964
Denomination Roman Catholic
Listing Grade II*

'I have tried to produce a building in which a large number of parishioners – six hundred – can participate in the celebration of Mass in circumstances which recall something of the intimacy of the Last Supper', Goalen claimed in 1963. This explains the theatrical, fan-shaped plan and raked floor.

The plan is based on two hexagons, each 12m (40ft) wide and covered by an umbrella vault supported on a single column. The sanctuary has two smaller umbrellas. Goalen believed that a church should reflect the glory of God in every element, particularly in the use of light. Money was insufficient for stained glass all round the church, so Goalen provided for it over the altar and entrance, and devised louvres for the other windows to give a subdued, even light. The *dalle de verre* is by Patrick Reyntiens, depicting the crown of thorns superimposed over tree symbols from the New Testament.

Elain Harwood

St Mary's Priory Church

Architect Jerzy Faczynski of Weightman and Bullen
Location Leyland, Lancashire
Year completed 1964
Denomination Roman Catholic
Listing Grade II

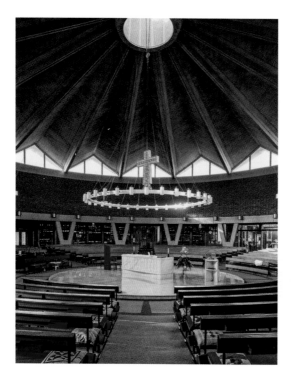 

Leyland in the 1950s was prosperous and expanding; a new church was needed for a growing congregation. Parish priest Fr FitzSimons, impressed by new liturgical architecture visited on the Continent, planned a 1000-seat church with a central altar. The Polish architect Jerzy Faczynski prepared the design. Adam Kossowski created the striking ceramic entrance tympanum and a hanging cross. Radical Liverpool sculptor Arthur Dooley's Stations of the Cross, Patrick Reyntiens's *dalle de verre* windows, George Thomas's inscriptions and Faczynski's tapestry together create a powerful composition of light, colour and intimate worship. Side chapels and a freestanding bell tower complement the drum. St Mary's design and furnishing was the vision of Fr FitzSimons, reflecting his Benedictine intelligence and contemporary Continental church architecture: a French or Swiss Roman Catholic sacred capsule landed in Leyland.

Aidan Turner-Bishop

St Matthew

Architect Robert Maguire and Keith Murray
Location Perry Beeches, Birmingham
Year completed 1964
Denomination Church of England
Listing Grade II

This is the second church by Maguire and Murray, built to serve a low-density
suburban parish of semi-detached houses. Into this unpromising landscape
the architects have set a great hexagonal box, of pale brickwork streaked with
horizontal bands of concrete, a squat tower combining sanctuary with belfry. There
are lower extensions to this box, so that it appears to tumble to the ground like a
fractured expressionist iceberg. The roofs are delicate, tipped-up planes, and sit on
mullioned clerestories. Go inside, and you see why. The hexagon appears to have
been truncated, with the off-centre altar set against the long, blank entrance wall.
The banded brickwork folds in on itself, becoming a cascade of tall concrete beams
that form a spiralling motion aligning altar, lectern and font. The congregation
is gathered 'naturally' around the clergy, bathed in toplight, and organised by a
complex but effortless geometry that serves to centre and unite.

Gerald Adler

St Patrick

Architect Gillespie, Kidd and Coia
Location Kilsyth, Lanarkshire
Year completed 1964
Denomination Roman Catholic
Listing Category A

The level of architectural invention in this church, attributed to Isi Metzstein and Miroslav Lutomski, verges on the bonkers. One side is solid brick with a slot for the entrance and curved projecting chapel wall; the other has transparent glass slices cut through hollow brick piers. A copper-clad upside-down roof perches over a sliver of glazing. One wall is gouged with channels inside, while through the thickness of the piers on the right the glass steps backwards and forwards. A concrete choir gallery involves a row of semicircles that cantilever out beyond the wall over glass lunettes. There is a lot of Le Corbusier, a hint of Scandinavian sixties churches, even a bit of Louis Kahn (sketches for his Unitarian Church at Rochester were published in *Architectural Design* just as Kilsyth was designed). Obsessively absorbed and transmuted, precedents hardly matter in this extraordinary composition in brick, concrete, glass and wood.

Robert Proctor

Holy Redeemer

Architect George Pace
Location Acomb, York
Year completed 1965
Denomination Church of England
Listing Grade II

At Holy Redeemer, Pace combined rectilinear tracery and thick concrete walls with medieval stonework from St Mary, Bishophill Senior, demolished in 1959. Amongst the salvage were many carved stones, including a Norman doorway of c.1180 and an arcade comprising round arches from 1180 and pointed arches of c.1350. The altar cross incorporates fragments of C9 or C10 work, also from St Mary's.

Pace's own contributions are among his most assertive works, including a coffered plaster ceiling, long chunky pews and a sturdy, vat-like font. It is also a bold declaration of the new liturgy, the client Reverend Wilkins explaining at the church's opening that 'the grouping together of altar, font, pulpit, lectern, prayer desk, etc… is intended to show that the ministry of both the word and the sacraments are of equal importance, and all take place in view of the people, who themselves are participants in them all'.

Elain Harwood

William Temple Memorial Church

Architect George Pace
Location Wythenshawe, Manchester
Year completed 1965
Denomination Church of England
Listing Grade II

This is one of Pace's most radical and liturgically imaginative designs. Yet the building is little more than a rectangular brick shed with rolled-steel joists and girders left exposed. The external envelope of brick – economic and honest – is pierced by Pace's trademark multiplicity of smallish vertical windows, with numerous dormers pointing from the roof.

The interior is organised on the diagonal with a modest free-standing altar in the corner furthest from entrance. Seating is arranged in two blocks at right angles to each other, and the focus on the essential sacraments is emphasised by placing the font in front of the altar and the bishop's throne behind. The choir is tucked away at the back on salvaged nineteenth-century pews. The new fittings confirm Pace's commitment to simplicity yet quality and craftsmanship – a solid-oak altar, concrete font and wrought-iron fixtures – overtly of their time yet simultaneously timeless.

Judi Loach

St Jude

Architect Lionel A.G. Prichard and Son
Location Wigan, Greater Manchester
Year completed 1965
Denomination Roman Catholic
Listing Grade II

At first sight St Jude's seems like a concrete drum in an ordinary estate; but step inside. The fan-shape interior has exposed concrete beams, infilled with warm brick, enclosing a top-lit sanctuary, enriched with a large mosaic Crucifixion. The Crucifixion, designed by Hans Unger and created by mosaic artist Eberhard Schulze, was the pair's first large-scale religious mural. Unger also designed posters for London Transport and the Post Office.

The mural's rich expressionism imbues the altar with a solemn intensity. The interior is surrounded with six tall windows of symbolic panels in vibrant *dalle de verre* glass designed by Robin Riley who wrote that the thickness of the glass and intensity of the colour quality 'and the notion that contemplation and quest are valuable human traits' prompted the decision to make the images in the windows many times life size.

Aidan Turner-Bishop

CATHEDRAL CHURCH OF THE HOLY SPIRIT

Architect Edward Maufe
Location Guildford, Surrey
Year completed 1966
Denomination Church of England
Listing Grade II*

Edward Maufe won the competition to build a new Anglican cathedral at Guildford in 1932. The site chosen was on the top of Stag Hill, a bleak lump of clay to the west of the town. Maufe designed the building to fit the site, with an almost pure cubic form and unbroken straight lines, having a long horizontal volume and a tower rising as a single mass from the highest point. He wanted the building to grow naturally out of Stag Hill itself and relied on proportion of mass, volume and line rather than elaboration and ornament.

Two of the conditions of the competition were that at least 1,500 people should be able to see the High Altar, a new departure for a cathedral, and that the cost should not exceed £250,000. To enable this to happen, Maufe did not spend money on wide aisles. He decided to have only passage aisles, raising the aisle arches up to soar out at the same level as the nave arches, thus achieving height and spaciousness and making flying buttresses unnecessary. This gave the cathedral almost one-third more internal space than a typical mediaeval cathedral. The cost limit meant that building in stone was out of the question, but Maufe brought back a brick from Albi Cathedral in southern France which he much admired, and the local brickworks made a similar brick out of the clay of Stag Hill itself.

Maufe believed that a church building should be a symbol expressing the Christian creed in all its parts and therefore the whole fabric of the cathedral should express religious truth in symbolic language. He said that 'the church is a sanctuary, not an assembly room: her people are not spectators, but are part of the church'. Maufe was a passionate believer in quality for his churches, and thought all forms of art could be

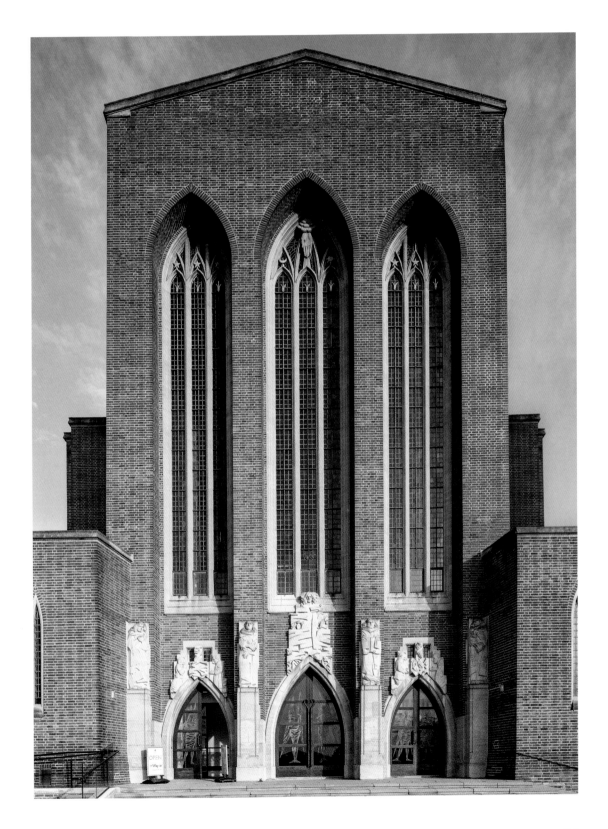

brought into the service of religion by employing artists of the first rank to execute the sculpture, wall paintings, metalwork and woodwork that would be needed. The dove and flames of the Holy Spirit are among the many symbols carved, painted or made in stained glass throughout the building. But there is less stained glass than might be expected as Maufe preferred to let natural light come in and illuminate the shapes of the pillars and arches. Thus his essentially plain design was brought alive by symbolic details to achieve a sumptuously simple setting.

Edward Maufe and his wife Prudence were key to the successful completion of the cathedral, paying the salary of a fundraiser for ten years. Prudence Maufe organised the embroidery of the wonderful kneelers, as well as designing many details of the vestments and embroidering the Bishop's mitre herself. The cathedral was dedicated on 17 May 1961, almost 30 years after the competition had been won, and Edward Maufe returned for the anniversary service every year until his death, wearing his favourite scarlet and pink Belfast Hon. LLD gown.

Juliet Dunmur

Swedish Mission Church

Architect Bent Jörgen Jörgensen with Elkington Smithers
Location Rotherhithe, London
Year completed 1966
Denomination Lutheran
Listing Grade II

Opened by Swedish King Gustaf Adolf VI, the Swedish Seaman's Mission is a fabulous showcase for 1960s Scandinavian design and craft. The entrance door, clad in copper sits next to the *dalle de verre* coloured glass wall by Christer Sjogren of Lindshammar glassworks, an exemplar for the Swedish glassmaking industry. Watch out for the original copper lettering on the front façade, and the giant free-standing anchor in the forecourt.

Inside, the bespoke copper lights, font and altar, were designed by the architects and shipped from Sweden. The use of high-quality teak, oak, limestone and exposed concrete stands out in the ground-floor spaces.

The building was designed for mariners involved in the timber trade overseas. It combined a re-modelled 1930s church with community facilities and a hostel. After the decline of the docks in the 1980s, the building remained a focal point for the Swedish community until it was sold in 2012.

Henrietta Billings

Craigsbank Church

Architect Rowand Anderson, Kininmonth and Paul
Location Edinburgh, Lothian
Year completed 1966
Denomination Church of Scotland
Listing Category A

Located at the end of a cul-de-sac in the Edinburgh suburbs, Craigsbank Church
is an arresting sight. The church has windowless, white-harled walls as tall as the
neighbouring houses. At one corner, the entrance is dramatically marked by a tower
whose curved form recalls Le Corbusier's chapel at Ronchamp.

The church is essentially square in plan and is almost entirely top-lit. The
congregation sits in tiers of raked seating around three sides of the sanctuary,
reflecting a modern approach to Scottish Presbyterian church planning which had
earlier found expression at St Columba, Glenrothes. At the same time, the layout
was intended to evoke the conventicle church gatherings which took place in the
seventeenth century in the hillside hollows south of Edinburgh.

The church was refurbished by LDN Architects in 2012. It demonstrates how
architectural drama can successfully be combined with liturgical focus.

Alistair Fair

St Peter's Seminary

Architect Gillespie Kidd & Coia
Location Cardross, Argyll
Year completed 1966
Denomination Roman Catholic
Listing Category A

St Peter's Seminary may be the only building in this compilation that is better known
for its history of dereliction than as a working religious settlement. Serving their
original purpose for only 14 years after completion, and subsequently being briefly
re-used as a drug rehabilitation unit, the buildings then entered a prolonged period
of abandonment and progressive destruction by a combination of vandalism and the
elements. At the same time its designers Izi Metzstein and Andy MacMillan moved
from active practice into teaching at the Mackintosh School in Glasgow, acquiring
cult status as architectural educators and critics. St Peter's, now listed at the highest
grade, has been the subject of innumerable failed rescue attempts. The failure of an
exciting project by local arts charity NVA and Avanti Architects to secure funding has
thrown into further doubt the future of St Peter's – already British modernism's most
spectacular and erudite ruin.

John Allan

METROPOLITAN CATHEDRAL OF CHRIST THE KING

Architect Frederick Gibberd and Partners
Location Liverpool
Year completed 1967
Denomination Roman Catholic
Listing Grade II*

Rising up the steps from Hope Street towards the entrance to Liverpool Metropolitan Cathedral, you are met with a powerful composition of abstracted forms and intersecting geometries. Like a modernist Wells, the west front projects away from the vast cylinders of the nave and the lantern and is adorned with Bill Mitchell's stylised vision of Golgotha and his intense and curiously lovable depictions of the Apostles. Set high on the ridge that it shares with Sir Giles Gilbert Scott's Anglican masterpiece at the other end of Hope Street, Frederick Gibberd's cathedral still awes me every time I see it.

That the artwork and architectural form are so harmonious at the entrance illustrates what lies at the heart of this much-loved but very often maligned building. Like Spence's Coventry Cathedral before it, Liverpool has

been handed down to us as a great vessel of post-war art and design and both are colourful jukeboxes of the primary talents of the period. But where Coventry wears its modernism politely and in places arguably only skin deep, Gibberd's building shows us the bare bones – its 16 immense ribs being the primary structural component both inside and out. Parts of the building are crude, but the assuredness in the overall form and the manner in which it creates the spaces for the artistic embellishments, remain Gibberd's central achievements.

The brief had bordered the impossible – deliver a new cathedral, retaining the partly built Lutyens' crypt, for a million pounds inside 5 years. It did not deter the profession and just under 250 entries came in from across the world, each one, in retrospect, more outlandish than the last. Gibberd's design was a shoe-in

and it re-established his credentials as a radical modernist. It also reflected a forthcoming seismic shift in liturgical practices. A cathedral fully in the round, to bring the clergy and the laity closer together, with a central sanctuary top-lit by the largest, continuous, *dalle de verre* window in the world. This was the 1960s, it was Liverpool – surely anything was possible.

It has swaggered, colourfully, through its first fifty years, inspiring wonder and controversy. Its distinctive shape has evoked at least two hypocorisms, 'The Mersey Funnel' and 'Paddy's Wigwam'. It is unique in world architecture but it's just as important as a homecoming beacon for Liverpudlians.

There's really no experience in UK architecture to compare with stepping into the nave for the first, or even the fiftieth time. The floor, the work of artist David Atkins, defines the positioning of the furniture and fans out in bands of concentric light and dark marble across the vast circle of the nave. Vertical stripes of rich red and ice blue lights define and mark each of the 15 chapels and entrances that ring the central space. Above the aluminium ciborium, a vast drum of coloured light contrasts with the bleak, dark acoustic tiles of the nave ceiling. Liverpool is a complete work of art, even if it remains a flawed piece of architecture.

Jon Wright

ABOVE The interior of Liverpool Metropolitan Cathedral, a view which opens up immediately as you step inside.

Mortonhall Crematorium

Architect Sir Basil Spence, Glover and Ferguson
Location Edinburgh, Lothian
Year completed 1967
Denomination Multi-denominational/multi-faith
Listing Category A

At Mortonhall, Basil Spence was determined to build 'the best crematorium in Britain'. Within a landscape that evokes Gunnar Asplund's Woodland Cemetery, Stockholm, the complex comprises two linked chapels, set above the 'working' part of the crematorium. Externally, the chapels have a strongly expressionist character. Pyramidal rooflights rise above angled walls of concrete blockwork, between which, at the south end of the larger chapel, are narrow bands of coloured glass, only fully seen and appreciated as one turns to leave.

The chapels' plain side walls are not only animated by a constant play of daylight but also serve to concentrate attention on the catafalque, which is bathed in light from concealed windows to each side and above. Simple benches and domed lampshades strike a Scandinavian note.

Alistair Fair

St Laurence

Architect Ralph Covell of Covell Matthews Partnership
Location Catford, London
Year completed 1968
Denomination Church of England
Listing Grade II

Known variously as the 'Mod' or the 'space-age' church on its completion in 1968, St Laurence is notable for both its distinctive, open-work spirelet and its octagonal, exposed concrete roof.

The interior of the main church is dominated by the bold triangular pattern of the reinforced-concrete octagonal roof structure. This rises up above a clerestory band of abstract stained-glass windows supported by slender concrete mullions, and is topped by a metalwork corona. Bespoke pews fan out from the altar. The main church is complemented by the subsidiary, pentagonal Lady chapel – which bears the spirelet – and by an adjacent community centre.

With many of its original features still intact, St Laurence gained a Grade II listing in 2010. Refurbishment of the roof and stained-glass windows was completed in 2017.

Kelley Christ

St Augustine

Architect Desmond Williams and Associates
Location Grosvenor Square, Manchester
Year completed 1968
Denomination Roman Catholic
Listing Grade II

The warm, richly conceived interior is hidden behind an austere facade. Set back from
Oxford Road, the square-plan church seems inconspicuous alongside the adjacent
Gothic art school, Georgian buildings, and Manchester Metropolitan University's later
All Saints Building. The entrance front is sculptural with central steps framed between
a bold forward projection, with a ceramic plaque and four full-height fins. The brick is
dark brown contrasting with bright Mancunian terracotta.

Brick continues inside this early manifestations of post-Vatican II liturgical thinking.
The interior is top-lit between the Vierendeel trusses, while Whitefriars *dalle de verre*
fills the recessed nave windows. Wooden benches are arranged so that all can see and
participate. The sloping timber ceiling emphasises sightlines and the view is terminated by
Brumby's awe-inspiring ceramic mural of *Christ in Majesty*. Close collaboration between
Brumby and Williams ensured art and architecture complemented each other here.

Diana Coulter

St Margaret of Scotland

Architect Williams and Winkley
Location Twickenham, Greater London
Year completed 1969
Denomination Roman Catholic
Listing Grade II

One of the first and most significant new churches in London designed and built after the Second Vatican Council, St Margaret of Scotland still conveys the optimism and openness of outlook of the 1960s. Designed by Austin Winkley of the practice of Williams and Winkley, the Church occupies the site of one of a series of ten, early-19th-century villas, only one of which still survives close by.

Whilst set back some distance from the road on the original building-line of the villas behind an unprepossessing car-parking area, the church has a particular architectural significance – not so much for its grey, concrete-blockwork walls, extensive flat roofs and Profilit glazing – but for its sheer architectural coherence, its sound and inclusive liturgical planning and the spatial delights of the principal worship space and the lesser spaces – complemented by Patrick Reyntiens's stained glass and Stephen Sykes's hanging cross above the altar.

Paul Velluet

St Thomas More

Architect Richard Gilbert Scott
Location Sheldon, Birmingham
Year completed 1969
Denomination Roman Catholic
Listing Grade II

Richard Gilbert Scott designed St Thomas More so that a membrane of abstract stained glass by John Chrestien wraps around the seating area and the stepped ceiling seems to float above it. This perfect balance of massiveness and lightness and the resulting lantern-like character of the building mean that despite its brutalist style, it captures some of the Gothic spirit for which the family of its architect was known. The diamond-shaped skylight above the sanctuary casts a beam of daylight over the altar below, giving dramatic focus to the space. Sky-lit bare brick side chapels recall Eero Saarinen's chapel at the Massachusetts Institute of Technology. The fan-shaped plan is a response to Vatican II and brings the congregation forward to surround the altar. On the exterior, two concrete fins soar from the centre of the roof, an appropriately aeronautical motif for a church located not very far from Birmingham Airport.

David Frazer Lewis

1970 &
After

St Andrew

Architect Alison and Hutchison & Partners
Location Livingston, West Lothian
Year completed 1970
Denomination Roman Catholic
Listing Category B

St Andrew's was the first Roman Catholic church to be completed in the new town of Livingston, between Glasgow and Edinburgh. It was designed by George Kennedy of Alison and Hutchison & Partners, a notable Scottish modernist practice.

Essentially circular in plan, the exterior presents a series of overlapping curved walls of board-marked concrete. One of these walls thrusts dramatically skyward, forming a 'spire' of sorts and signifying the church's presence. The top-lit interior is more delicate than one would expect from the robust concrete exterior. Curved white walls are combined with a boarded timber ceiling whose pattern and rising height focus attention on the altar.

The design of the church embodies the liturgical reforms of Vatican II in its emphasis on the relationship between priest and congregation. Although it has been altered, it retains much of its original character.

Alistair Fair

Mid-Glamorgan Crematorium

Architect Maxwell Fry of Fry, Drew, Knight, Creamer
Location Coychurch, Bridgend, Mid-Glamorgan
Year completed 1970
Denomination Interdenominational
Listing Grade II*

Maxwell Fry felt cheated when his mother was cremated in a banal, uninspiring crematorium and was impressed by the funeral ceremonies he witnessed working in India. He first addressed the need for an 'anatomy of mourning' through an emotive modernism in a lecture to the Cremation Society in 1964, where he impressed local dignitaries looking to build a crematorium at Coychurch.

Fry provided a consolatory atmosphere through two means. His crematorium and Chapel of Remembrance are embedded into the language of the region through reused local stone, and a harmonious landscape employs a sweeping ceremonial drive, drifts of trees and an eye-catching lake fronting the main chapel, Capel Crallo. A broad entrance canopy and cloister features glass by local students. A concrete cowl (removed in 1993) and overhanging cushion-like roof acknowledged Le Corbusier's chapel at Ronchamp. The secondary Capel Coity is concealed in the woods, denoted only by its copper roof.

Elain Harwood

Marychurch

Architect Mather & Nutter
Location Hatfield, Hertfordshire
Year completed 1971
Denomination Roman Catholic
Listing Grade II

This striking circular church is neither large nor especially progressive but is pleasingly well-detailed, and dominated by the intense coloured glass of Dom Charles Norris of Buckfast Abbey. It was designed as early as 1963 by George Mather, and resembles a domesticated Liverpool Metropolitan Cathedral, with brick and concrete castellated piers divided by slot windows, tile-hung prow marking the sanctuary, and ornamental aluminium flèche. Unlike Gibberd's building, however, the altar is off-centre and the congregation sit beneath a dome and glowing oculus. *Dalle de verre* windows were intended as integral from the start and Norris was approached in 1967. His jagged diagonals represent the Jesse Tree in graduated colours from yellow to dark blue; the Evangelists look on from behind; pastel shades make the Lady chapel lighter; spinning globes of sacramental grace fly around the strange font; day and night (life and death) mark the entrances.

Robert Proctor

St Joseph

Architect Anthony Jaggard of John Stark & Partners
Location Wool, Dorset
Year completed 1971
Denomination Roman Catholic
Listing Grade II*

It would be easy to overlook this building. Funded by the Welds of Lulworth Castle
to respond to Wool's westward expansion, it hunkers down, fortress-like. Rectangular
in plan with a low narthex, the north and south walls, graduated and rendered,
are punctuated by plum-brick semi-circular towers with exaggerated waterspouts,
emphasising the apex of the shallowly pitched roof.

Inside the fortress theme continues in small details in the towers containing the
baptistery and Blessed Sacrament chapel. St Joseph's strength is its space-frame roof,
providing a large, light worship area. The mesh of aluminium tubes resembles a
20th-century vision of a delicate stone vault. The altar is top-lit by the pyramidal
lantern supported on thicker aluminium at its base, drawing attention upwards.
The lateral progression of 'beams' is counterbalanced by longitudinal light fittings
throwing light up to the trusses and down over the felt-lined concrete benches.

Diana Coulter

CATHEDRAL OF SS PETER AND PAUL

Architect Ronald Weeks of Sir Percy Thomas Partnership
Location Clifton, Bristol
Year completed 1973
Denomination Roman Catholic
Listing Grade II*

Clifton Cathedral claims to be the first cathedral in the world to accord completely with the liturgical guidelines issued by the Vatican in November 1963. These sought to involve the congregation by permitting the Mass to be celebrated in modern languages and for the celebrant to face the people.

Clifton Cathedral is more successful than Liverpool because it places the top-lit sanctuary to one side, facing a fan of seating for the congregation so the celebrant can see everyone at once. The result is a hexagonal space, and hexagons and equilateral triangles became the basis of the whole design. Reinforced concrete made possible the broad spans and became a feature of the decoration. The hierarchy of the internal spaces is marked by a rising ceiling height, from the low entrance and baptistery into the main worship space, subtly lit by rooflights

and rising to the three-part thrusting spire, presumably symbolic of the Trinity. Colour is limited to the entrance, where a screen wall of *dalle de verre* glass by Henry Haig leads to the baptistery and shields first views of the main space. There, William Mitchell carved the low-relief Stations of the Cross in wet concrete, with just 1½ hours to complete each one before it set. The Portland stone font is by Simon Verity.

Built in a remarkably short time to a low budget (£600,000), the rough wigwam-like exterior does not prepare one for the quality of the interior. There, Clifton achieves a rare integration of materials and spatial quality, combining serenity and simplicity with craftsmanship in the concrete detailing.

Grace Etherington

Our Lady of Lourdes

Architect McCormick Tracey Mullarkey
Location Steelstown, Derry
Year completed 1977
Denomination Roman Catholic
Listing Grade B2 (equivalent Grade II)

'Space, light and form – these are not expensive elements', commented Liam
McCormick, Ireland's most important modern church architect, in the year that
the church at Steelstown was completed. It is one of few churches designed by
McCormick for an urban setting, and is considered a 'pair' with his church at
Glenties, for both are dominated by a striking tent-like roof. It is dramatic, almost
primitive in its simplicity, on a simple longitudinal plan, constructed in economic
materials that reflect the architect's intention to be 'socially correct', in its context.
Light flows though narrow strips over stepped divisions, recalling the traditional
division of liturgical space. The landscaping serves to sensitively embed the church
in its surroundings. Several of McCormick's favoured team of artists are represented,
including Patrick McElroy, Helen Moloney and Oisín Kelly.

Delia Graham

LIVERPOOL CATHEDRAL CHURCH OF CHRIST

Architect Sir Giles Gilbert Scott
Location Liverpool
Year completed 1978
Denomination Church of England
Listing Grade I

Giles Gilbert Scott won the competition to design Liverpool Cathedral when he was 22 years old. It was to be the first Church of England cathedral built on a new site since the Reformation. The city of Liverpool was thriving on Atlantic trade, and more than anywhere else in Britain, commercial buildings swelled toward the proportions of American skyscrapers. Conceived, in a sense, as a giant village church for a giant village, the cathedral would have to be large enough to reflect its importance in the skyline. Ultimately, it would be the largest church in the United Kingdom.

Scott's design, the broad lines of which he finalized in 1910, was highly Romantic. His chief aims were gloomy light and a sense of mass: 'It is either an engine of emotion, or it is nothing,' the architect and critic H.S. Goodhart-Rendel wrote. With its enormous central tower bracketed by transepts, the cathedral had a nearly symmetrical composition – a highly unusual arrangement.

The publication of Liverpool Cathedral's design had immediate global impact in the first decades of the 20th century. Summarising its effect, the head of the Liverpool School of Architecture, C.H. Reilly, wrote that 'There is no need to lay stress on how it has influenced current church building. At a stroke, as it were, the latter seemed to come to life again after a sleep of half a century or more […] Scott, more than anyone else, broke the archaeological shackles and convinced churchmen that one could be modern and creative.' The American architect Bertram Grosvenor Goodhue wrote that Scott's design was revolutionary because it did away with the pinnacles and crockets that were a standard feature of Gothic work. Instead, it proclaimed its steel structure with cubic masses and clean lines.

Inside, the rather short nave is screened from the rest of the cathedral by an arched bridge, and the massive crossing, which opens into the transepts and chancel, is the primary seating space for the congregation. Mirroring the natural rise of the ground, each portion of the space – nave, crossing and chancel – has a higher floor level and is more brightly lit than the space that precedes it, creating a clear progression from entrance to altar. Scott liked to refer to Liverpool Cathedral as 'Space Gothic', a term originally coined by an American visitor, because it captured the fact that spatial effect was a primary concern.

Liverpool Cathedral was a total work of art in a way that was rare for 20th-century British cathedrals. Whereas Westminster Cathedral was created as a shell to be decorated by later artists in varying styles, from the beginning Liverpool had a team of artists who designed every fitting, vestment, sculpture and service leaflet.

Sir Giles Gilbert Scott died in 1960, and the Cathedral was completed by members of his office using fibreglass specially cast to look like the existing stonework. The cliff-like, nearly windowless west end designed by Scott was unfortunately never built. Instead, a simplified west end was completed to the design of Scott's former chief draughtsman, F.G. Thomas.

David Frazer Lewis

ABOVE Liverpool Cathedral, looking up under the central tower between the pairs of transepts, completed in 1942.

St John Ogilvie

Architect Clunie Rowell with Douglas Niven and Gerard Connolly
Location Irvine, North Ayrshire
Year completed 1979
Denomination Roman Catholic

Built as part of the Bourtreehill neighbourhood in Irvine New Town, the church of St John Ogilvie was intended to be a landmark in an evolving townscape and to promote the formation of a new community. It is located adjacent to a shopping precinct and a contemporaneous Church of Scotland parish church, the Relief Church (by Hay Steel and Partners).

The two churches face each other across a narrow pedestrian plaza, sharing a language of concrete blockwork and angled forms. St John Ogilvie is octagonal in plan, with the tiled roof rising in two stages to a pyramid. Chunky wooden details complement the solidity of the blockwork, both inside and out. Within the church, a complex timber roof structure re-interpreted the structural experiments of historic religious architecture, while omnipresent square grid patterns situate the design within the Mackintosh revival of the 1970s and '80s.

Alistair Fair

Robinson College Chapel

Architect Gillespie, Kidd & Coia
Location Cambridge, Cambridgeshire
Year completed 1981
Denomination Interdenominational

Robinson College is a megastructural melange made of 1.4 million handmade red bricks, out of which the chapel rises like a jagged iceberg, crystallised from the same ever-present bricks. Robinson is simultaneously a robust and radically modernist statement, but is also within an essentially medieval tradition of combining spaces for protection, learning, sleeping, eating and worship. The benefactor, David Robinson, had wanted something more traditionally neo-Gothic for the chapel, but was won round by the inclusion of John Piper and Patrick Reyntiens's huge stained-glass window. The stone-lined interior is centred on this window, depicting the sun as Glory of God, with light depicted bursting dazzlingly through foliage. It is framed by a window in the shape of an inverted stepped ziggurat, one of many playful patterns reminiscent of interwar Amsterdam School architecture. The chapel is daringly inventive, while also evoking older forms infused with an intense spirituality.

Otto Saumarez Smith

St Mary

Architect Cullinan Studio
Location Barnes, Greater London
Year completed 1984
Denomination Church of England
Listing Grade II*

The fire that partially destroyed St Mary's, Barnes, in June 1978 was at the time
a disastrous blow to the parish. Yet it produced one of Edward Cullinan's finest
buildings that, in his own words, 'takes a complicated built history and powerful
local feeling as inspiration, not as encouragement to nostalgia and pastiche'.

In origin a modest village church, St Mary's had been submerged under a dull
Victorian rebuilding which reduced the original church to a mere aisle. Led by a
charismatic priest, the parish backed Cullinan's proposal to remove the 19th-century
additions and create a new place of worship, light, flexible and responsive to new
visions of the liturgy. Old and new are seamlessly brought together under a great
open timber roof, reminiscent of Bernard Maybeck's church at Berkeley (a building
Cullinan loved) and equally of the great tithe barns of medieval England. St Mary's
embodies the idea of a living tradition fundamental to Cullinan's art.

Kenneth Powell

St Mary Magdalen

Architect Francis B. Roberts
Location Penwortham, Preston, Lancashire
Year completed 1988
Denomination Roman Catholic

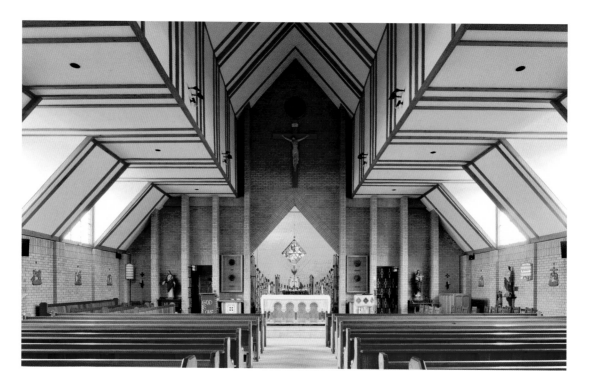

Roderick Gradidge, one-time vice-chairman of the C20 Society, declared this 'the best church of the decade'. Roberts had worked quietly for local modernists BDP before establishing a reputation for Arts and Crafts work, a historicist post-modernism. A commission to build a new church for his own parish gave him the opportunity to set up his own practice.

St Mary Magdalen began as a chapel of ease by local architect Wilfred Mangan in 1911–12, which Roberts retained as a church hall at right-angles. Glass from the old church was brought into the link between the old building and the new, which is similarly of brick, but with sweeping roofs and a pyramidal tower. The simple interior, with its dominant ceiling, is enlivened by sanctuary gates by Giuseppe Lund and J.H. Edge, and an east window by Mark Angus representing the story of Whitsun. The altar came from the old church.

Elain Harwood

Fitzwilliam College Chapel

Architect MacCormac Jamieson Prichard
Location Cambridge, Cambridgeshire
Year completed 1991
Denomination Interdenominational

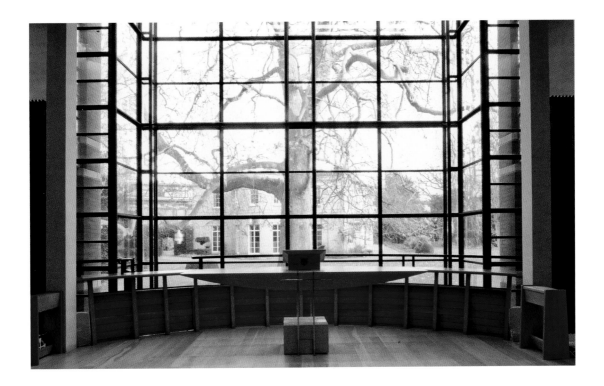

Luminous white concrete and smooth oak characterise Fitzwilliam College's chapel.
It won multiple accolades including the David Urwin Award for Best New Building
in 1993. Denys Lasdun's original master plan for the modern college in the 1960s
featured a chapel at the heart of a spiral design. Without sufficient funding however,
the college waited nearly three decades for its worship space. MJP Architects, who
had worked with Fitzwilliam since the 1980s, designed a chapel in the round with
flexibility, musical performance and contemplative devotion in mind. Richard
MacCormac's curving design references the hull of a ship, with strong associations
of salvation and community. The grid structure of the east window suggests a cross,
indeed a multitude of crosses, as it frames a characterful plane tree, whose seasonal
changes and bucolic steady vitality respond contrastingly to the sleek white textures
of MJP's surfaces.

Ayla Lepine

Cathedral of St Mary and St Helen

Architect Erith & Terry Architects
Location Brentwood, Essex
Year completed 1991
Denomination Roman Catholic

The most notable ecclesiastical manifestation of the 1980s classical revival, and
the first purpose-designed classical cathedral to be built in England since Wren's St
Paul's, Gilbert Blount's Gothic revival church of the 1860s was raised to cathedral
status in 1917, and considerably enlarged with modern additions by Burles Newton
& Partners in the 1970s. These lacked the 'numinous' quality desired by Bishop
Thomas McMahon, so he commissioned Quinlan Terry's replacement classical
design, which mixes Italian and English Renaissance influences. Every detail and
every item of furnishing is the result of the close collaboration between architect
and patron. In its liturgical planning, with a central altar designed for maximum
congregational participation, the cathedral lies within the mainstream of post-Vatican
II Catholic church design, as realised in very different form at Liverpool Metropolitan
Cathedral. But here the glazing is clear and all the classical orders are present.

Andrew Derrick

St Paul

Architect Peter Jenkins of Inskip & Jenkins
Location Harringay, London
Year completed 1993
Denomination Church of England

Unusually among architects, Inskip & Jenkins specialise in both conservation and new work. St Paul replaced a Victorian Gothic church destroyed by fire in 1984. Smaller than its predecessor, it still needed to have prominence, and places a tall equilateral triangular roof, constructed in steel and clad with zinc, sailing over brick diaphragm walls. 8m-high triangular windows ensure the white interior is well lit from above. Sculptor Stephen Cox designed the altar, carved from Egyptian porphyry, a travertine reredos, the font and stations of the cross.

Although seen by some as an example of post-modernism, Jenkins is adamant that his is not a style-based approach. He describes St Paul's as a neo-rational temple with skins of brick referencing Gottfried Semper's theory that the origins of walls as enclosing structures were fences and animal pens.

Catherine Croft

Abbey Church of Our Lady Help of Christians

Architect Francis Pollen
Location Worth, Sussex
Year completed 1989
Denomination Roman Catholic
Listing Grade II

Many visitors descending the steps that lead into the Dominican monastery and school at Worth are surprised at the grandeur of Francis Pollen's church, the outcome of a design process begun in 1961. A late convert to Modernism after growing up under the mantle of Lutyens, Pollen succeeded in merging the two strands with utter conviction. Although funds were not lavish, the keynotes are massive brick piers supporting the ring beam, light spilling down a flared concrete funnel from a lantern into a regular space that is almost impossible to capture in photography. Pollen wrote 'I believe that churches must feel as if they had just happened as a result of divine laws of geometry, mechanics and proportion, timeless laws.' His friend, the stained-glass artist Patrick Reyntiens told him he had 'produced singlehanded a style that has reference to the past and can give hope to the future'.

Alan Powers

Cathedral Church of St James

Architect S.E. Dykes Bower
Location Bury St Edmunds, Suffolk
Year completed 2005
Denomination Church of England
Listing Grade I

The diocese of St Edmundsbury and Ipswich was created in 1913, and in the following year John Wastell's church of St James, Bury St Edmunds, was selected as St Edmundsbury Cathedral. In 1945 Stephen Dykes Bower was appointed for enlarging the building, a task which was to occupy him for the rest of his life – he died in 1994 – reaching its culmination in 2005 with the completion of the crossing tower. Dykes Bower had no articled training, but he was greatly influenced by F.C. Eden, a former pupil of G.F. Bodley. Dykes Bower's elegant, if not sublime, style at St Edmundsbury enhances Wastell's work, imparting a harmony superbly complemented by a series of fixtures and fittings in limed oak and magnificent stained glass by A.E. Buss of Goddard & Gibbs. Indeed, Dykes Bower created at St Edmundsbury a building where one can worship 'in the beauty of holiness'.

Julian W.S. Litten

Lumen URC

Architect Theis and Khan Architects
Location King's Cross, London
Year completed 2008
Denomination United Reformed Church

A striking new 8-metre window, featuring a spiralling bronze screen by Rona Smith, now announces to the street this formerly reticent 1960s brick church in Bloomsbury. Asked to create spaces for a café and community use by those of any faith, Theis and Khan inserted a dramatic white cone into the heart of the building, a concrete shaft of light piercing its full height, to provide a place for private worship or reflection. A circular window casts ever-changing light within and around this sculptural form, drawing attention to the church's structure of angled concrete trusses.

The 'sacred space' separates a café overlooking the street from the body of the church, oriented towards an existing stained-glass window, re-located to the south wall. A font, drinking fountain and fountain for the new cloistered garden were commissioned from Alison Wilding. Wrapped around the garden is an extension housing three rooms for community use.

Susannah Charlton

Bishop Edward King Chapel

Architect Niall McLaughlin
Location Ripon College, Cuddesdon, Oxfordshire
Year completed 2013
Denomination Church of England

Five miles from Oxford, but in a village, adjacent to Victorian Gothic buildings by G.E. Street, this chapel was the gift of the Sisters of Begbroke marking their relocation to the theological college. An intricate Glulam timber structure of tapered columns creates an ambulatory around a slightly sunken oval space, with a lectern and an altar at its two focal points. The lattice recalls gothic vaulting or a forest canopy, and the ring of clerestory windows gives views to the interlacing branches of adjacent trees. A top-lit prayer room, a bay for private prayer, and a niche for a tabernacle, project from the ellipse, which is clad externally in textured Clipsham limestone. Precedents include St Michael, Frankfurt, by Rudolf Schwarz, 1954, and Seamus Heaney's poem 'Lightenings viii', was also a source of inspiration. McLaughlin says the project marked 'the arrival of a more artless confidence' for his practice and reflects that, 'sometimes you have to just step back and say this is really enjoyable. It's why I became an architect.' It shows.

Catherine Croft

Stanbrook Abbey

Architect Feilden, Clegg, Bradley
Location Wass, North Yorkshire
Year completed 2015
Denomination Roman Catholic

Stanbrook Abbey is an exemplar of contemporary monastic architecture. Rising out of the North York Moors, the site blends austere geometry in the orthogonally planned living quarters with gentle timber curves in the Abbey church. The architects worked closely with the nuns who were keen that the design should reflect an emphasis on nature in their spirituality. This has been achieved by creating synergies between eco-technology, local materials and use of the picturesque. From within, the buildings offer uninterrupted vistas of the national park, while externally, long grass feathers into the stone and timber facades, making the structures appear rooted in the landscape.

The church is shaped internally by the natural light that sweeps around it throughout the day, creating a different visual setting for each of the nuns' five daily offices. Though the community chose a modern design, they are aware that the surrounding moors are dotted with the remains of numerous medieval abbeys.

Kate Jordan

Places of Worship in a Changing Faith Landscape

KATE JORDAN

In the 20th century, successive waves of migration – particularly from the Commonwealth – have tempered Christianity's domination over Britain's faith landscape. While traditional Christian congregations have seen a general picture of decline, other forms of worship have climbed, transforming the towns and cities of Britain with the diverse and creative architecture of world faiths. The rise of personal spiritualities has also seen the emergence of new typologies such as retreat centres and multi-faith spaces.

Before 1914 the only minority religion to have made an impact on the British landscape was Judaism. Jewish migration to Britain peaked around 1900, when Ashkenazi Jews fled the pogroms of central and Eastern Europe and joined the longstanding Sephardi community from the Iberian peninsula. Most synagogues were characterised by a Moorish orientalism expressed in polychromatic brickwork and cupolas, which had evolved by the 1920s into a Byzantine style. Examples are found in the synagogues designed by Marcus Glass, a first generation Lithuanian immigrant, in Sunderland, Newcastle and Clapton, where the trend is expressed in their polychromy and mosaic decoration.

Eastern styles were also applied to a small number of Islamic buildings. Muslims settled in Britain in growing numbers after the First World War, with early mosques found in homes and adapted buildings. Shah Jahan Mosque in Woking was the first mosque built in Britain, a personal project of the dilettante Hungarian Jew Gottlieb Leitner in 1889, designed mainly to host visiting Indian dignitaries. The first mosque to be built by a British community was the Fazl Mosque in South London built for Ahmadi Muslims by Thomas Mawson and completed in 1926. It shares only a general orientalism with the Shah Jahan Mosque – indeed, externally the Fazl Mosque has little more in common with Shah Jahan than it does with contemporary synagogues.

In Europe the International Style was considered an appropriate language for Judaism by the 1930s, but British Jews were more reticent and only a handful of modernist synagogues were built. The most striking example is Owen Williams's 1938 synagogue at Dollis Hill – an angular concrete building adorned only by a pattern of hexagonal and inverted-arch windows. The congregation were unhappy with the result, partly because it was over-budget and partly because they took exception to the radical aesthetic. History has been kinder: the historian Sharman Kadish calls it 'an isolated, if technically flawed, example of truly original modernism in British synagogue architecture'.

The early 20th century also saw the arrival in Britain of quasi-religions that straddled secularism and spirituality. Rudolf Steiner's

Anthroposophical Society, which described itself as a 'spiritual science', had no use for formal places of worship but its architecture was nevertheless deeply invested in belief systems. Steiner's arcane architectural theories inspired Montague Wheeler's expressionist designs for Rudolf Steiner House in London, built in 1924-32.

The number of places of worship for all faiths increased dramatically after World War II. Large-scale migration from the Indian subcontinent following partition was reflected in increasing numbers of Sikh gurdwaras, Hindu, Buddhist and Jain temples, and mosques. Growing South Asian communities established worship spaces in private homes and repurposed buildings, including former chapels, in industrial centres across Britain but particularly in London and the Midlands.

The Holocaust stimulated a break with the past for European Jews, who now fully embraced modernism as the language of Jewish architecture, a shift powerfully expressed in Thomas Hancock's designs for the Jewish boarding school and synagogue at Carmel College completed in 1965. Communities found ways to express the trauma of the Holocaust by turning away from Europe and looking towards Israel and the United States for inspiration. Like other post-war synagogues, the Brighton Reform Synagogue is a dedicated Holocaust memorial with stained-glass windows by John Petts, depicting diaspora and persecution. These are companions to those Petts designed for a new church in Birmingham, Alabama, demonstrating a political empathy between Reform Judaism and the black civil rights movement. The synagogue itself, completed in 1968 to designs by Dennis Sharp Associates, draws inspiration from

Walter Gropius's 1960 Temple Oheb Shalom in Baltimore. Judaism has since declined, partly through migration, and today the pressing issue is to protect its heritage from demolition; the former synagogue in Brick Lane, London, has become the Jamme Masjid mosque.

Of the few purpose-built commissions that were undertaken in the 1970s, the most significant was the Regent's Park Mosque. Attempts to build a non-denominational mosque had been fomenting since the beginning of the 20th century and, with financial backing from the British Government, a formal committee was founded in 1944 to oversee the building. Questions of style were much debated as British Muslim communities were ethnically and culturally very diverse. The debate was settled when the King of Saudi Arabia donated £2 million towards the project. Frederick Gibberd won an open competition with a design that blended British modernism with traditional Arabian motifs, an approach which was considered pastiche by his detractors and drew wide criticism from the architecture world.

The established South Asian communities, now including second and third generation migrants, have invested greater funds in their buildings since the 1970s. Domes and minarets added to adapted buildings engraved the presence of increasingly confident migrant communities on to the landscape. In Leicester the Jain community purchased an empty Victorian church in 1979 and had by 1988 added a traditional Jaisalmer stone facade and dome from Rajasthan, and remodelled the interior with hand-carved marble, limestone and timber components prefabricated in Gujarat. The result was an authentic Hindu

ABOVE London Central Mosque, Regents Park, 1969–78 by Frederick Gibberd and Partners.

temple, at the time of completion the largest outside India. A similar application of traditional styles and techniques is seen in the Wat Buddhapadipa Buddhist Temple in Wimbledon, a complex of buildings commissioned by the Thai community. Opened by the King and Queen of Thailand in 1982, it has become a place of pilgrimage for Buddhists from all ethnic backgrounds on account of its culturally faithful architecture and narrative murals produced by Thai artists. Similar examples in the UK include the NKT Tibetan Manjushri Centre in Cumbria and the Tibetan Stupa in the Himalayan Garden at Harewood House near Leeds.

In their purpose-built projects, Sikhs and Hindus have continued to use traditional building methods and styles, as at the Sri Guru Singh Sabha gurdwara in Southall, opened in 2003 at a cost of £17 million. The Shri Sanatan Hindu Mandir in Wembley is an architecturally perfect Hindu Temple, which opened in 2010 having taken sixteen years to build. Other communities have begun to explore stripped-down or abstracted versions of traditional styles and to commission projects from major international architects such as the Cambridge Mosque by Marks Barfield and John McAslan's proposed redevelopment of the Morden Mosque in South London. Shahed Saleem and John Stebbing have taken this approach further by stripping out all traditional architectural features and producing simple box designs for mosques and a synagogue respectively, which reveal their identity only through abstract motifs. Waugh Thistleton Architects have employed a

ABOVE Bushey Jewish Cemetery, Bushey, Hertfordshire.
RIGHT Vajrasana Retreat Centre, Walsham-le-Willows, Suffolk.

truly transcultural minimalism in Jewish prayer halls at Bushey Cemetery, where the bare rammed-earth walls converse more expressly with nature than with traditional worship.

Here is an architecture directly responding to shifts in worship and spirituality: the blank, culturally anonymous syntax of the Bushey prayer halls was applied by Peter Zumthor to his Secular Retreat in Devon, commissioned by Alain de Botton for Living Architecture as a space for meditative reflection. Similar, too, is Walters and Cohen's Vajrasana Retreat Centre, completed in 2016. The centre is an offshoot of the London Buddhist Centre financed by a bequest from the fashion designer Alexander McQueen, and is designed to accommodate a liminal space between

prayer, meditation and personal development. It has considerably more in common with the objectives of Living Architecture than it does with traditional Buddhist approaches. An emerging trend in faith spaces is that many appear to be contracting into zen-like nothingness, as new spiritualities become untethered from physical space. Sharman Kadish has observed among younger generations of Jews, 'a psychological return to rootlessness, to the portable tradition of the tent sanctuary'. Elsewhere, 'white cube' interiors, such as Herzog & de Meuron's new multi-faith room at Tate Modern – a space somewhere between art installation and place of worship – are intended to be mute, so as not to disturb the private conversation between worshipper and worshipped.

Stained Glass

JANE BROCKET

Historically stained glass is a very slow-moving art, and until the end of the 19th century, change in Britain happened at a very gentle pace. Since 1914, however, the story of ecclesiastical stained glass has been packed with development and variety. It is possible to divide the century of stained glass into three periods, that up until the Second World War, thence until the 1970s and from that point until today.

By 1914, stained-glass design, which had become rather dull and tired, was on the cusp of change. Alfred Wolmark's 1915 window in St Mary Slough is now often cited as the sign of the missed opportunity for stained-glass artists to take the medium in a new direction. Influenced by German expressionism, purely abstract, colourful and daring, it was much closer to what was happening in the contemporary, experimental art world than that of ecclesiastical art. This is the window that influenced Lawrence Lee, Geoffrey Clarke and Keith New when they were planning their nave windows for the new Coventry Cathedral. That it took more than thirty years for Wolmark's window to be recognised as the turning point illustrates just how much stained glass was on hold until after the Second World War.

Instead, the First World War intervened, and stained glass stalled. Many churches and donors looked backwards and returned to the chivalrous, conventional, saintly and historical, and to copies of sentimental, popular paintings such as James Clark's *The Great Sacrifice* (1914). Nevertheless, some superb stained glass was made by Arts and Crafts makers under the powerful leadership of Christopher Whall, and influential teaching of Henry Payne at the Birmingham School of Art. Highlights include the explosive, almost mystical, windows of Karl Parsons such as those in St Laurence, Ansley, and the beautiful book illustration-style glass of Louis Davis in pure, brilliant colours, as in St Martin, East Woodhay. These contrast with the figurative, pale, pretty and polite windows by prolific designers such as Martin Travers, Ninian Comper and Geoffrey Webb.

The 1920s and 1930s also produced some excitingly new and different windows by artists immersed in contemporary art trends. Douglas Strachan's dramatic, Vorticist style can be seen at its best in Winchelsea. J.E. Nuttgens' Eric Gill-influenced linear, woodcut style adapted brilliantly to suit both small windows as in St John the Baptist, Windsor, and monumental

LEFT St Etheldreda, Ely Place. East Window. Glass by Joseph Nuttgens, 1952.

ABOVE, LEFT St Mark, Broomhill, Sheffield. Detail of East Window illustrating the Te Deum, glass by Harry Stammers, c.1963.
ABOVE, RIGHT St Mary, Stoke Newington. Glass by W.T. Carter Shapland, 1960.

windows as in St Etheldreda, Ely Place, London. Leonard Walker's swirling, vibrant, semi-abstract windows exploit the qualities of the material itself. They are made with exceptionally beautiful glass and resemble paintings by Klimt; there is a stunning example in Holy Trinity, Hartshill.

20th-century stained glass is unusual in the field of large-scale, public – and permanent – art in having so much work by women. Christopher Whall offered equal training and working opportunities to female artists, and many went on to use the facilities at the Glass House in Fulham, set up by Mary Lowndes of Lowndes & Drury in 1906. This studio-workshop arrangement enabled many talented makers to flourish, and helped women to work

independently. As a result, makers such as Margaret A. Rope and her cousin Margaret E. Aldrich Rope, Florence Camm and Trena Cox took glass painting, portraiture, colour choice and glass selection to new levels of brightness and beauty, and frequently included local and contemporary details, while the Irish artist Wilhelmina Geddes made a handful of unusually powerful windows for English churches which reflect her unique artistic vision.

In the end it took a second world war to provide the decisive break with tradition. The need for windows in damaged, rebuilt or new churches offered an unexpected and unparalleled opportunity for a real revival of the art which took the form of a mostly ad-hoc, local approach, with John Piper the only major artist working in the medium. The post-war period boasts a glorious mix of abstract, semi-abstract, figurative, contemporary and traditional by designers with different backgrounds. Many were skilled in several disciplines and media such as illustration, lettering, woodcut, linocut, watercolour, oil painting and poster design, and brought elements of these into their windows. However, most of the excitement, buzz and publicity around stained glass was inevitably generated by the art schools themselves and the artists who trained there. For a brief moment in the late 1950s and early 1960s, church stained glass was regarded as a cutting-edge, even glamorous, art.

This was mostly due to the windows made for the new Coventry Cathedral. The trio from the Royal College of Art who were responsible for the stunning nave windows – Lawrence Lee, Geoffrey Clarke and Keith New (plus assistants) – plunged into abstraction which was then dominating public debate, as did John Piper and Patrick Reyntiens with their slightly later baptistery window. Although it can sometimes overshadow the subject of post-war glass, Coventry is a superb place to begin an examination of the subject together with the windows of three of the period's most innovative and experimental makers.

Elsewhere, the traditional figurative style continued but was recast in bright, sometimes cinematically brilliant Technicolor colours by makers such as Christopher Webb, Francis Skeat and Hugh Easton. They frequently set their figures on clear backgrounds, probably as much due to limited budgets and reduced availability

of materials as artistic choice. This approach was also popular with makers of memorial windows. Hugh Easton was the artist of choice for Royal Air Force memorials and his delicately painted, camp, blond angels and handsome servicemen can be found in many places, including the Battle of Britain window in Westminster Abbey, St George's RAF Chapel at Biggin Hill, and St George's Centre, Chatham. There could be no greater contrast to his windows than the chunkily leaded, Cubist-influenced east window in Eton College Chapel by Evie Hone, the Irish artist who is for many, the pre-eminent post-war stained-glass maker, and who beat Easton to the commission. Yet even the conventional mode was being updated and figures were now often modelled on real people in contemporary clothes. Excellent 'everyday saints' in their uniforms can be seen in Bristol Cathedral, where Arnold Robinson paid tribute to the efforts of volunteers and civilians during the war, and in the Civilian Acts of Mercy window by Nora Yoxall and Elsie Whitford in Birmingham Museum & Art Gallery.

The post-war period also features windows by a number of lesser-known but brilliantly talented designers who deserve recognition for the contribution to making stained glass a modern, relevant art. Harry Stammers marries saintly and secular with his superb draughtsmanship and illustration, mix of incidental and architectural detail and grisaille, and modern colour (often a cheerful Festival of Britain palette), plus genuine affection and gentle humour. He was George Pace's favoured stained-glass artist and examples of their collaborations can be seen in St Mark in Broomhill, Sheffield, and St Martin le Grand in York. Harry Harvey, who worked in Stammers's

ABOVE, TOP Christ Church, Southwark. Glass by Frederick Walter Cole, 1960. **ABOVE, LEFT** Sheffield Cathedral. Glass by Harry Harvey, 1967. **ABOVE, RIGHT** Shrewsbury Roman Catholic Cathedral. Glass by Margaret Agnes Rope, 1929.

York studio and was also helped in his career by Pace, updates his mentor's clear, direct style for the 1960s and 1970s with vivid colours, skilful lettering and areas of beautiful abstract glazing instead of plain quarries. Many of his windows are in Yorkshire churches. Leonard Evetts, a supremely talented designer and letterer, developed a distinctive style as evidenced in his masterpiece scheme in St Nicholas, Bishopwearmouth, and his windows in the North East of England. The rebuilt churches in the City of London, with an immense concentration of excellent post-war glass, provide a comprehensive collection of windows by lesser-known artists, amongst them John Hayward's windows at St Mary le Bow and St Michael Paternoster Royal with dense leading, elongated, Henry Moore-influenced figures and a mass of fascinating detail. Elsewhere there are windows by Lawrence Lee, Brian Thomas, Christopher Webb, Hugh Easton, A.K. Nicholson Studios, Carl Edwards and A.E. Buss.

The late 1950s and '60s saw the introduction of *dalle de verre* (slab glass) for church windows. The technique of setting thick, chipped and faceted glass in concrete or resin had been developed in France in the 1930s. In the right hands, *dalle de verre* can be stunning, and it marries brilliantly with the concrete of many post-war Catholic churches in new estates and towns, for example the charming windows by Gabriel Loire in St Richard, Chichester, the wonderful abstract walls of glass by Henry Haig in Clifton Cathedral, and the calm, pale, columns of glass by Margaret Traherne in the Chapel of Unity in Coventry Cathedral.

Stained glass has always reflected the era in which it was made, and in the 1960s it kept pace with contemporary visual culture and captured something of the decade's excitement and energy surrounding technology and progress. Atomic patterns, planets, telescopes, petri dishes and microscopes appeared in windows, most notably in the 1960 window by W.T. Carter Shapland in St Mary, Stoke Newington, which includes the Jodrell Bank telescope. Windows also mirrored social changes, and occasionally a touch of Socialist Realism can be found. F.W. Cole's 1961 scheme in Christ Church, Blackfriars, confers a dignity and heroic status on local carpenters, bakers, printers, office workers, char-ladies and builders constructing London County Council housing, all of whom are depicted in fascinating contemporary detail.

By the late 1960s and early 1970s, the rate of commission was slowing down. The psychedelia and flower power of the Seventies largely bypassed stained glass – a missed opportunity judging by the few examples of the style by the likes of Rosemary Rutherford in Suffolk. In the 1980s highlights are fewer and farther between. Instead, stained glass again started to move in a new direction, the culmination of which can be seen in Millennium windows.

Churches now began to include less overtly religious subjects, preferring instead for windows to appeal to the community both inside and beyond the Church. As a result, they tend to contain images of local history, landscape, landmarks, trades and work, in collage or photo-album-style montages of scenes designed by local artists and even local schoolchildren. The messages and narratives are simple, colourful, child-friendly and carefully inoffensive – but not mould-breaking. This makes it all the more

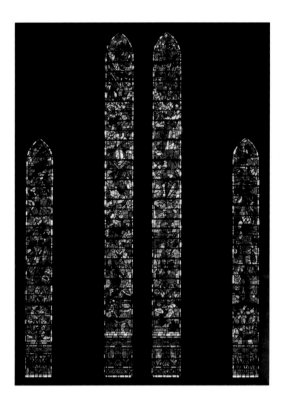

ABOVE, LEFT St Mary, Slough, West Window. Glass by Alfred Wolmark, 1915.
ABOVE, RIGHT St Richard, Chichester. Glass by Gabriel Loire, 1958.

satisfying when you do come across a window which is exciting or different, for example fine, experimental windows by the likes of Mark Angus and Derek Hunt, the later work of John Piper and Patrick Reyntiens, for example in Robinson College Chapel, Cambridge, and the renowned scheme by Marc Chagall in All Saints, Tudeley.

The Millennium may prove to be the last hurrah for stained glass, as spare money is now more likely to go on repairs and reordering. As a result, the Millennium provided a good moment to review the condition of English stained glass. It is generally very nice, safe, pleasant and colourful, more secular than deeply religious, no longer sermonising or didactic but more celebratory

and inclusive. There are some stunning windows which give cause for optimism, such as that by Rachel Thomas in St Paul, Birmingham, and the window by Christopher Fiddes and Nicholas Bechgaard at St Nicholas, Potterspury. Since then intriguing stained glass has been made by artists such as Thomas Denny, Helen Whittaker, Benjamin Finn, Ann Sotheran and Meg Lawrence, who all have a recognisable style that they express clearly and confidently.

Taken together, the windows made between 1914 and 2014 reveal that English churches have a superb and permanent collection of 20th-century art and design, yet its stained glass is still a vastly underrated form of visual culture and public art.

Art & Artefacts

ALAN POWERS

Beyond the fixed elements of a building and its glass a church depends for its historical interest and effectiveness on a great many other things, making up the apparatus of seating, preaching, reading and the celebration of the sacraments at the font or altar. As H.S. Goodhart-Rendel explained, in the middle ages 'a church undecorated was just a church unfinished, a church not ready for use'. The 20th century, at least from 1914 onwards, experienced several waves of what the church historian, artist and former Benedictine monk, Peter Anson (1889–1975) called, *Fashions in Church Furnishing*, the title of what remains probably the best history of the subject. As John Betjeman wrote, 'Mr Anson's book is really not at all about a trivial subject. It may be a bit specialist and it may shock some by being so entertaining', yet, as he went on to explain, it carries youw to the heart of belief in any historical period. Experience sadly shows that too many parishes and clergy intent on re-orderings or simply bored with the overfamiliarity of their surroundings, and too often supported by DACs and encouraged by architects, continue to consider these elements trivial. While the whole history of 20th-century design in all denominations is still emerging, the actual evidence, much of it rare and special, is at constant risk of destruction or neglect.

A speeded-up film of history would show the catastrophic destruction of church art in the Reformation followed by episodes of reversal culminating in a spate of new furnishing in the Victorian period, and then a new cycle of 'the stripping of the altars', to use Eamon Duffy's phrase. Even in one country and one denomination, the story of all these things is a complex one. The subject includes at least as much work done within older buildings as in new ones. One story concerns a refinement of knowledge of the past as a justification for its present use and creatively interpreted by the artist. A key instance was the reintroduction of the 'English altar' by John Ninian Comper at St. Wilfrid, Cantley, near Doncaster, in 1893, resulting from careful attention to mediaeval illuminations, a more rigorous version of the research and practice of Pugin marking the opening of a new phase in the Gothic Revival. These altars had curtains hung three sides round from carved and painted 'riddel posts'. They were enthusiastically copied, becoming the symbol of a certain kind of high-church worship, known as 'The English Use', popularised through successive editions of *The Parson's Handbook* by Percy Dearmer. The Warham Guild was a supply company founded by Dearmer and his associates to replace poor-quality late-Victorian fittings with alternatives, and responsible for the proliferation of English Altars.

J.D. Sedding and other Victorian rebels reintroduced Renaissance classicism in the

1880s, the first stirrings of what became the 'Back to Baroque' movement in the Edwardian period and beyond. Comper justified mixing classical and Gothic as 'unity by inclusion', based on ancient precedents, but it also played to a counterfactual fantasy, that the Reformation had never happened and classical fittings had simply accreted as an extra layer in Gothic churches, or, as Betjeman put it in describing an outstanding example of this approach at Blisland, the architect F.C. Eden 'made a Cornish church as it would have been had there been no Victorians to wreck it and no Puritans to smash its ornaments'. Full-on Baroque invaded the Anglo-Catholic stronghold of St. Mary, Bourne Street, much of it by the designer Martin Travers, a glass artist with a penchant for gilded plywood, seen in Butterfield's St Augustine, Queen's Gate and his own original church at Carshalton. The 1930s brought a different but equally theatrical taste for Art Deco fittings, such as the chrome reredos at St. Gabriel, Blackburn, by F.X. Velarde or the streamlined fittings and scalloped curves of Bernard Miller at churches such as St Columba, Anfield, which was often referred to as 'The Essoldo, Anfield', as if it were a cinema.

These entertaining experiments in taste were conducted against a background of what Cyril Pocknee called, 'badly designed, uninspired and badly produced' furnishings, against which Francis Eeles set up the system of Diocesan Advisory Committees, under the Central Council for the Care of Churches; while they may have prevented the worst from happening, they were also accused of stifling the best. In an average C of E church, as Betjeman wrote in 1958, one would expect to find a children's corner 'with its pale reproductions of watercolours by Margaret W. Tarrant, the powder-blue hangings and unstained oak kneelers'. Everything, he went on to imply, was too tame and too small in scale. Against safe 'good taste', there was counter-movement involving Kenneth Clark and George Bell, Bishop of Chichester, whose actions included mounting the exhibition 'The Artist and the Church' in 1944, curated by John Piper.

This promoted the idea that artists rather than craftsmen were needed to bring fresh thinking and energy. As Piper wrote in the catalogue, 'The artist, if he is a good artist, must be a craftsman as well. The craftsman, if he is freshly creative, and only if he is so, will be an artist.' Thus, the next revolution aimed at large-scale, strong colour and the expressive language of modernism, with a tendency to refer to the early history of the Church. As the Scottish architect Esme Gordon put it, 'We of to-day seek and see parallels in the more formative times rather than in full-flowering ages'.

With their magazine, *L'Art Sacré* (1936–1954) the Domincans Marie-Alain Couturier and Pie-Raymond Régamey established a groundwork that was influential across the denominations in Britain. Glass was one of the major means of expression and Couturier made news by commissioning Fernand Léger to create glass at Audincourt, while tapestries and mosaics also flourished. In England, Coventry Cathedral, opened in 1962, acted as a showcase for lettering, tapestry, mosaic and sculpture in the new Continental manner, earning such derisory descriptions as 'a pavilion of ecclesiastical art' or 'a ring-a-ding God-box' for its pains. The plain wooden chairs at Coventry, developed by R.D.

ABOVE, LEFT 'Modernistic Baroque' line drawing from *Fashions in Church Furnishings 1840–1940* by Peter F. Anson.
ABOVE, RIGHT St Protus and St Hyacinth, Blisland.

Russell and his colleagues, were, however, widely adopted and continue to be produced.

Bishop Bell is especially associated with encouraging modern church murals, mostly in older buildings, by artists including Hans Feibusch, a German émigré whose works include murals in the crypt of St. Elisabeth, Eastbourne, added to a recent church during the war on the theme of the *Pilgrim's Progress*. These have long been under threat, but owing to patient negotiations by the Twentieth Century Society, have a chance of being relocated to a suitable building nearby when the church is demolished. Other artists who worked for Bell included Alan Sorrell and Augustus Lunn, but the most famous

example will always be the combined work of Duncan Grant and Vanessa Bell at Berwick, also painted during the war. Cathedrals rather than parish churches most commonly commissioned modern sculpture, although the Rev. Allan Wyon was in the unusual position of being a sculptor who was ordained and held the living of St. Peter, Newlyn, where he employed Martin Travers to add baroque touches to a Gothic Revival interior, and added a fine white marble Madonna and Child. The most famous exception, however, is Walter Hussey's commission to Henry Moore for a Madonna and Child at St. Matthew, Northampton, in 1944. The stone-carving school of Eric Gill gave way to the cast bronze

of Elisabeth Frink, but stone returned in work by Tim Crawley and others at Westminster Abbey. Carved figures by Rory Young at York, Southwell and St. Albans have continued to reverse the expressionist trend with delicate but arresting naturalism.

While the work of individual artists attracts attention, the majority of architects working during the period expected to design a range of fittings for their own churches and, more numerous, the churches where they were called in to re-order or redecorate. Comper continued working up to his death in 1960, and Stephen Dykes Bower, in many ways his successor, remained active into the 1980s, contributing solid but finely-tuned altar crosses and candlesticks to many churches, tactfully clearing away rubbish and often adding brilliant colour to organ cases and monuments and vestments and altar frontals stitched in a continuation of Victorian practice. For him, what mattered was the harmonious relationship of space, light, colour and detail, closer to the effect of flowing counterpoint than of declamatory music. From this viewpoint, modern art of the kind promoted by Walter

Hussey as Dean of Chichester, such as the work of Piper, Graham Sutherland or Chagall, appeared attention-seeking and disruptive to architectural cohesion, although for many people it made the church more approachable. George Pace represented an in-between style, with his transcription of Gothic into straight lines and right angles.

The post-war decades also saw a notable revival of church silver, encouraged by the Goldsmiths' Company, with work by Leslie Durbin, Louis Osman and others. Keith Murray, who went into partnership with the architect Robert Maguire, was one of a new generation of designers and makers of church artefacts, predominantly in metal.

Even today, the aesthetic assumptions behind much church art and decoration have changed little since the 1950s, broadly following the post-war 'School of Paris', symbolic in often simplistic ways and straddling the line between representation and abstraction, with emphasis on texture and surface. Although now within a historic tradition itself, this attitude disclaimed earlier historical forms as 'pastiche'. Yet, as Esme

ABOVE, LEFT Ralph Beyer lettering on St Paul's Church, Bow Common.
ABOVE, RIGHT Altar at St Gabriel's Church, Blackburn, designed by F.X. Velarde.

Gordon suggested, 'should the work be based on sincerity and conviction the ring of truth can be heard resounding directly across the centuries'. Since the 1990s, however, conceptual art and installation have offered the opportunity to bring messages and meanings through a wider range of metaphor. Taking the form of temporary display, as with the video pieces of Bill Viola, the ephemerality of these pieces allows for greater risk-taking as well as the danger of simply buying into a well-known brand. Installations can create a sense of occasion and in the light of Esme Gordon's advice to parishioners, that 'as the acceptance of any gift implies that it will remain in the church *sine die*, care is necessary', they can depart and leave no trace behind.

Lettering finds a place in churches and churchyards and while much of it has been perfunctory, even before the computer put the means of production in the hands of non-experts, there is a distinctive British tradition of stone cutting, largely still in the classical line of Gill, although crossed over with the more expressive German tradition practised by Ralph Beyer at Coventry and also seen by many passers-by at St Paul's, Bow Common by Maguire and Murray. The Memorial Arts Charity has raised public awareness of this work, coaching clients and artists to achieve appropriateness without over-predictability, while the charity Art and Christianity Enquiry (ACE) prompts discussion through events, publications and awards.

Practice Profile:
Giles, Adrian & Richard Gilbert Scott

When G.F. Bodley died in 1907, Giles Gilbert Scott took over his rooms at Gray's Inn Square. He would operate a small office from Gray's Inn for the rest of his career.

The architectural historian John Summerson was one of Scott's pupils, and in his unpublished memoirs, Summerson recalled that Scott's office was 'homely and leisured... Scott himself I found to be a calm and tolerant man, with blue eyes and a boyish way of expressing himself. His main interest seemed to be golf.' Scott styled himself as a gentleman architect. He never employed more than eight people, and he was responsible for every element of the design himself.

Resulting largely from his fame as the architect of Liverpool Cathedral, Scott became one of the first truly international celebrity architects. He was knighted at age 44, became the youngest Royal Academician since J.M.W. Turner, and was elected President of RIBA during its centenary. Scott always said that his great love was designing churches, and these designs were his most radical and influential works. He built striking, revolutionary churches at Golders Green, Broadstairs, Northfleet, Bournemouth, Bath, the Isle of Man, Liverpool and in dozens of other places across the British Isles. Describing his church-building philosophy, Scott wrote that being able to create an atmosphere that inspired worship was 'a type of functionalism with which the functionalist is unfamiliar.' Scott understood the commodious and utilitarian bell-tower as landmark and source of music; the well-lit raised chancel as a theatre for the Eucharist; the gloomy, screened aisle chapel as a place for private prayer. Scott also consulted widely on church design, encouraging young ecclesiastical architects across the British Empire. Giles's brother Adrian Gilbert Scott was an important church architect in his own right. Although Adrian maintained an independent practice, the brothers acted as a team, with the gregarious Adrian helping to manage clients or assisting with major projects.

After the First World War, Giles Gilbert Scott also established specialties in industrial design and university buildings. Amongst the creations of his firm were Battersea Power Station, the London Guinness Factory, the K2 and K6 GPO telephone kiosks, Waterloo Bridge and Bankside Power Station. He rebuilt the chamber of the House of Commons. Unlike many architects with Edwardian roots, his non-ecclesiastical work was primarily urban and institutional; he did hardly any domestic work.

Scott's son, Richard Gilbert Scott, was made a partner of his father in 1949 and continued the firm after his death. He also succeeded to his uncle's practice. He developed a style that was more in line with post-war trends. The heavy concrete style of his London Guildhall Library and the Birmingham churches he designed at Sheldon and Tile Cross still managed to evoke the Gothic spirit. His later work included the Post-Modern Gothic London Guildhall Art Gallery, which was completed in 1999.

David Frazer Lewis

LEFT Lady chapel, Liverpool Anglican Cathedral, with G.F. Bodley, completed 1910.

ABOVE, TOP Our Lady Help of Christians, Tile Cross, Birmingham, 1966. **ABOVE** Our Lady Star of the Sea and St Maughold, Isle of Man, 1906–46. **RIGHT** Our Lady of the Assumption, Northfleet, Kent, 1913–16.

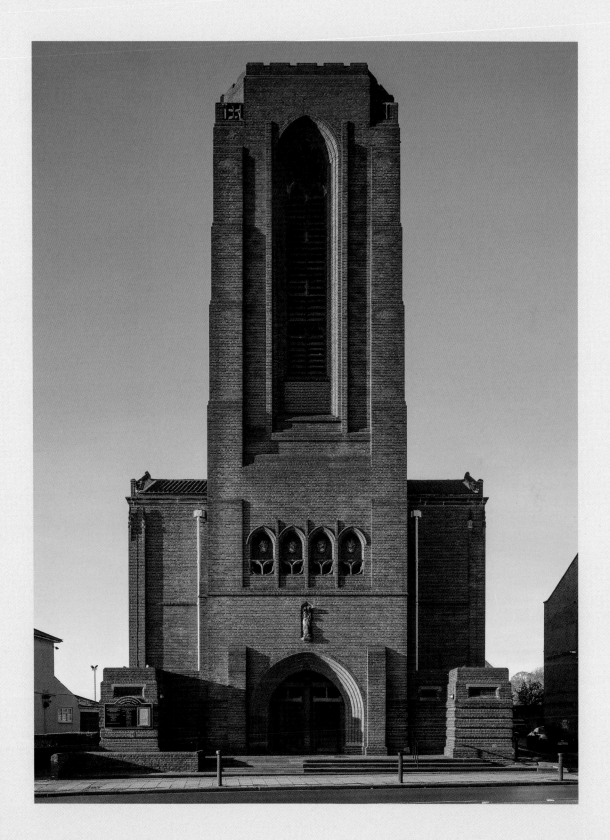

Practice Profile:
H.S. Goodhart-Rendel

Goodhart-Rendel (1887–1959) was a misfit, brilliant with words, accomplished in music and possessed of an encyclopaedic knowledge of Victorian churches at a time when hardly anyone else was interested. He was also an original and successful designer whose work has puzzled those who look at it. His best-known book, *English Architecture Since the Regency* (1953) was based on a series of lectures, for the one-hour paper. Epigrammatic, challenging and amusing, this was his preferred medium and he was a popular speaker. He was President of the RIBA in 1937–38 and seen at the time as a leader of the profession, although critical of the work of many contemporaries.

Taking his cue from the architects J.J. Burnet and Temple Moore, Goodhart-Rendel saw style as a relative issue. As he put it, 'A "style", traditional or modern, was a set of recognisable symbols by means of which an artist could convey his message to those he hoped would receive it with gratification. If its symbols were not exact and appropriate to the significances of which the artist had made them the vehicle, the style had been ill-chosen; if they were used without significance, or were such as to distract attention from the significance to the character of its vehicle, the style was noxious.' It was a position he demonstrated by working in a range of styles, sometimes approaching pastiche, and at others inventing freely, according to his sense of what was needed. Thus, he welcomed the use of steel-frame construction, but added abstract decoration to the cladding, sometimes with a nod to the Edwardians Halsey Ricardo and Beresford Pite.

His work at St. Mary, Graham Terrace, Pimlico (1922–36) was a series of intricate insertions in an existing Victorian centre of High Anglicanism. He enjoyed decorative design in bright colours – painted decoration and ceramic murals and reliefs.

St. Wilfrid, Brighton (1932–34) was Goodhart-Rendel's first major church, a manifesto for rational construction, sadly converted to flats in the 1980s. His later churches are more relaxed, including Holy Spirit, Ewloe (1938) and St Mary the Virgin, Hounslow East (1937–55) externally understated but internally complex in space. He was unusual as an architect whose work became progressively more assured as he got older, and after he converted in 1936, most of these were Catholic. Arguably his finest churches came at the end – Holy Trinity, Dockhead (1959–60), St. Francis and St Anthony, Crawley (1955–62) and Our Lady of the Rosary, Old Marylebone Road, (1958–62). These and other works form a coherent group playing on similar themes adapted from French Romanesque.

While Goodhart-Rendel was remembered as a writer, his later design work went largely unpublished in any magazines, and was forgotten until the centenary exhibition of his work at the Architectural Association in 1987. With the current revival of interest in coloured brick patterns, of which he was a pioneer revivalist, he seems especially relevant.

Alan Powers

RIGHT Lady chapel of St Mary, Bourne Street, Chelsea, 1922–36.

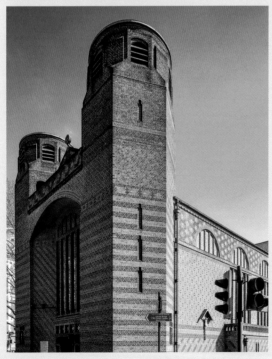

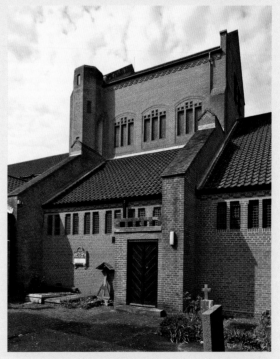

ABOVE, TOP St Wilfrid's, Brighton, 1932–34.

ABOVE, LEFT The Most Holy Trinity, Dockhead, 1957–60. **ABOVE, RIGHT** St Francis and St Anthony, Crawley, 1958–59.

ABOVE, TOP (LEFT AND RIGHT) Our Lady of the Rosary, Marylebone, 1959–63.
ABOVE, LEFT St Cecilia, Sutton, Greater London, 1954–59. **ABOVE, RIGHT** Sacred Heart, Cobham, 1955–59.

Practice Profile:
Edward Maufe

Edward Brantwood Maufe (né Muff) practiced from 1909 to 1969. He was born in Ilkley near Bradford, but his father, an admirer of Ruskin and Morris, moved the family south to Red House, Bexleyheath. Maufe entered into pupillage with London architect William A. Pite in 1899 while taking evening classes at the Architectural Association, with a period at St John's College, Oxford, studying Greek.

In 1910 Maufe married Prudence Stutchbury, later a Director of Heals, to form one of the most dynamic husband-and-wife partnerships of their era. His first major commission, Kelling Hall, Norfolk, was completed in 1914. His first church commission was for the Reverend Dick Sheppard, creating a social centre in the crypt of St Martin-in-the-Fields in 1914 (further work in 1924). These were followed by two innovatory churches for the deaf and dumb: St Bede, Clapham (1923–24) and St Saviour, East Acton (1924–26), both incorporating social facilities beneath a raised worship area, giving these churches a strong verticality and with special adaptations for the congregations such as raked floors and twin ambones (one for a sign reader).

Maufe's breakthrough came in 1932 when he won the competition for Guildford Cathedral on a new site outside the town. This huge commission was to dominate his career but problems with funding and a long wartime break in construction meant that it was only completed in 1965. He built a number of churches in the 1930s as practice-runs for Guildford, notably St Thomas, Hanwell, which combine Maufe's developing ideas on materials, decoration and use of space in collaboration with sculptors such as Eric Gill and Vernon Hill, Moira Forsyth on stained glass and his wife Prudence on textiles.

Maufe took over as chief architect to the Imperial (later Commonwealth) War Graves Commission after Lutyens's death in 1944, continuing the principles set after the First World War but adding his own imprint, most notably at Brookwood Military Cemetery and the Air Forces Memorial at Runnymede (1953). He also rebuilt the war-damaged Inns of Court in London, notably the libraries at Gray's Inn and Middle Temple. Maufe's major post-war church commission was St Columba's Church of Scotland, Pont Street completed in 1955 but he also made major additions to Bradford Cathedral. A sequence of simpler, more modernistic churches included St Mary Hampden Park, Eastbourne; St George, Goodrington (Torbay); and St Alphege, Edmonton.

What makes Maufe's churches special is their interior spatial planning and strong contrasts of bare wall and colour in the form of fresco and heraldic design, ceiling painting and use of textiles. They embody the best of Scandinavian early 20th-century design ideas and arts and crafts traditions and are instantly recognisable. Most, but not all, are listed. They are well-adapted for modern worship with no division between nave and chancel, mostly without pews, with ample provision of vestries and social space within the structure.

Robert Drake

LEFT St Saviour, East Acton, 1924–26, with twin ambones.

ABOVE, TOP-LEFT St Bede, Clapham, London, 1923. ABOVE, TOP-RIGHT St Thomas, Hanwell, Greater London, 1933–34, glass by Moira Forsyth. ABOVE, LEFT Cathedral Church of St Peter, Bradford, Yorkshire, 1951–65, ceiling detail. ABOVE, RIGHT St Alphege, Edmonton, Greater London, 1959. RIGHT Cathedral Church of St Peter, Bradford, Yorkshire, 1951–65.

Practice Profile:
Nugent Francis Cachemaille-Day (1896–1976)

Nugent Francis Cachemaille-Day (1896–1976) was probably the most groundbreaking ecclesiastical architect of the early 20th century in England, his work forming a bridge between the inter- and post-war periods. His earliest churches of St Nicholas, Burnage (1931–32), St Alban, Southampton (1933) and St Saviour, Eltham (1933–34) were designed with Herbert Welch and Felix Lander, a partnership he left in 1935. He designed or re-configured over 60 churches during his career.

Externally his churches are strong brick fortresses, redolent of Germanic architecture. Uncompromising and bold they made a statement of strength in a period of uncertainty and perceived secularisation. Yet inside, the churches are all about inclusivity and community. As early as 1947, long before the design of the pioneering St Paul, Bow Common, he had committed to print the need for proximity of altar and people: a concept which appeared in preliminary designs for several of his 1930s churches, but which he failed to execute. He understood that the barrier between true communication lay in the location of the choir. Cachemaille-Day sought a solution that kept the choir in a position to lead worship rather than separating it: this can be seen in his churches of St Paul, Ruislip Manor and St Winfrid, Testwood where he uses a transept, cruciform or square arrangement to locate the choir at the side of the altar. This occasionally caused conflict – the choir at St Michael, Wythenshawe were moved from an intended rear gallery to the traditional position after the intervention of the Bishop of Manchester.

Cachemaille-Day's careful use of colour and texture can be seen in the colourful ceiling decoration at St Nicholas, Burnage, the brick fins that continue from outside to inside at St Saviour, Eltham and the little golden gem of a chapel in St Michael's Clubhouse in Westminster, beautifully gilded in mosaic by Eric Newton, Cachemaille-Day intended similar decoration elsewhere: his description of the proposed apsidal end at St Paul, Ruislip Manor is indicative (never decorated due to accusations of extravagance).

Cachemaille-Day's post-war churches continued his careful consideration of practicality. He rebuilt bomb-damaged churches and designed new churches with a freer rein to execute his progressive designs, while maintaining his concerns for 'erecting less expensive churches without the sacrifice of permanence and architectural dignity'. All Saints, Hanworth and St Michael and All Angels, Hackney reprised the square design, and more ingenious solutions were achievable, such as arranging a hall at a right angle to become a second nave at St Richard of Chichester (sadly demolished), which followed a similar unexecuted design for St Mary, Becontree, in the 1930s. The relocation of St Anselm, Davies Street, to Belmont in Harrow (1939) and the rebuilding of St Thomas, Clapton Common (1958), show Cachemaille-Day's careful response to surviving fabric.

The prolific Cachemaille-Day deserves recognition for the quiet revolution he promulgated during the mid-20th century.

Clare Price

LEFT St Michael and All Angels, Wythenshawe, Manchester, 1937.

ABOVE, TOP St Saviour, Eltham, Greater London, 1933–34.
ABOVE St James, Clapham, London, 1958.

ABOVE, TOP St Barnabas, Tuffley, Gloucestershire, 1939–40.
ABOVE St James, Clapham, London, 1958.

Practice Profile:
F.X. Velarde

F.X. Velarde, 1897–1960, a protégé of Professor Charles Reilly at the Liverpool School of Architecture, visited Germany in the 1930s where he fell under the spell of Dominikus Böhm's expressionist churches. St Monica's, Bootle (1937) made his name. It has a towering brick westwork, with angels by Tyson Smith. Inside the brick continues with solemn arches and deep piers penetrated by the aisles, while the nave is flat with its beams painted green. Velarde did his own structural calculations, with unpredictable results; at St Monica's, the west-end arch needed an emergency steel truss, which resulted in a surprisingly elegant composite structure. He was pragmatic, once saying to his assistant, 'I don't want it to be too perfect.' Several stories have him drawing details on site, in the sand with his stick. (Velarde was injured in a car accident in 1932 and never fully recovered his mobility.)

After the war came a change: Velarde designed a dozen light-hearted and colourful suburban churches, most in the North West, two in London. They have a toy-like quality that speaks of the 1950s. Many have a campanile like a rocket.

St Teresa in Upholland, Lancashire (1957) is typical. The picturesque tower has little arches, a motif that reminded Pevsner of de Chirico. The brick volumes are easy to read because the wall surface is only perforated by small rounded openings. In fact, the south wall has no windows at all, only buttresses capped with angels looking over an area of paving sloping like a stage. Inside there is colour; ceilings are painted in huge blue or orange diamonds and there are squat gold mosaic columns with blue capitals. English Martyrs, Wallasey, St Teresa, Borehamwood, and St Luke's, Pinner, are equally stylish.

Velarde's effects were achieved with the same materials being used for shops and houses in post-war Britain: brick walls, tiled roofs, steel trusses, mosaic and painted plywood. Fundamentally his work is classical but there are no orders and he favoured slight asymmetry – usually there is only one aisle and lighting is predominantly from one side. Stained glass and lead work are gone; instead there is tinted glass in concrete window surrounds. Mullions were often cast-concrete angels; could he have been the last British architect to use the sculpted human form in his work? Other than that, decoration is sparing except for gold highlights; Velarde loved gold and often used it in the form of mosaic tiles.

At a time when it was belittling to say of an architect that they were a pattern maker, his ceilings were geometric grids: in an era of white modernism he used bold colour. To stand in the Lady chapel at Holy Cross, Bidston, is to bathe in blue. When architect and writer Robert Maxwell was a student, he heard him say, 'Mendelssohn was OK, Corb was not'.

Undiscovered architects, like undiscovered composers, are implausible, but Velarde might be just such a person and should be treasured as a true English expressionist.

Andrew Crompton

LEFT St Luke, Pinner, Greater London, 1957.

ABOVE, TOP-LEFT St Luke, Pinner, Greater London, 1957, ceiling detail. **ABOVE, TOP-RIGHT** Holy Cross, Bidston, Merseyside, 1959. **ABOVE** St Teresa of the Child Jesus, Borehamwood, Hertfordshire, 1961.

ABOVE, TOP (LEFT AND RIGHT) St Teresa, Upholland, Lancashire, 1955–57.
ABOVE St Matthew, Clubmoor, Liverpool, 1930.

Practice Profile:
Sir Basil Spence

Basil Spence was a romantic and individualistic architect in an age of teamwork. Born in Bombay, Spence trained at Edinburgh College of Art and spent his year 'out' in Lutyens's London office. Spence's childhood in India left him with an appreciation of the effects of light on three-dimensional forms, and his college years accustomed him to working with artists. With Lutyens he learned how to handle ceremonial design and the art of charming clients.

Spence joined William Kininmonth in partnership in 1931, developing a varied practice strong on private houses in a variety of styles. Wartime experience at the Camouflage Development and Training Centre at Farnham introduced him to artists and techniques, which served him well when he established himself after the war as a specialist in exhibition design. This was most evident in the Sea and Ships Pavilion at the 1951 Festival of Britain where he worked with sculptors such as John Hutton and Siegfried Charoux. In 1946 he established a new practice in Edinburgh, where he and his partners (Bruce Robertson, and later Hardie Glover and Peter Ferguson) attracted a wide range of commissions. Work in England came more slowly after he established a London office in 1948. For a time the practice specialised in schools and university buildings, despite winning the Coventry Cathedral competition in 1951. While the cathedral took shape, Spence designed 11 parish churches, experimenting with effects for use at Coventry. Those of the 1950s, although conventionally planned, deployed directional lighting, wall textures and clear glazing to generate drama. The simple designs made clever use of art within tight budgets. Later churches were more original and powerfully massed, notably St Matthew, Reading, with its diagonally positioned altar and the sculptural forms of Mortonhall Crematorium. His only university chapel to be built, the non-denominational Meeting House at Sussex (1965–67), had a circular plan lit by coloured glass panels arranged in chromatic sequence and an oculus in the roof. Spence kept up to date with the changing modernism of the 1960s through extensive travel and by listening to his young assistants.

After securing prestigious commissions for Sussex, the Rome Embassy and barracks at Hyde Park, Spence divided his practice into three, forming a personal atelier at his Canonbury home to focus on them, named Sir Basil Spence OM RA. Architects from the larger Edinburgh and London offices, respectively Sir Basil Spence, Glover & Ferguson and Sir Basil Spence, Bonnington & Collins, visited Canonbury at crucial stages in a design. Spence's non-doctrinaire attitude, an empathetic response to his clients, and encouragement of young architects produced a varied body of work. Criticism from conservationists of his late works, at Hyde Park and Queen Anne's Gate, and his position as an establishment figure obscured his achievement in creating powerful new forms and symbols for Britain's post-imperial identity.

Louise Campbell

LEFT St Catherine of Siena, Sheffield, 1958–60.

ABOVE, TOP Meeting House, Sussex University, 1965–67.
ABOVE, LEFT AND RIGHT St Chad, Coventry, 1954–57.

ABOVE, TOP St John the Divine, Coventry, 1954–57.
ABOVE Mortonhall Crematorium, Edinburgh, completed in 1967.

Practice Profile:
George Gaze Pace

George Pace (1915–75) was one of the most productive architects in post-war Britain, but as a church specialist, working mainly in the north and Wales, his work was little noticed.

Pace, however, considered himself to be more of a modernist than many of his contemporaries who were celebrated in the architectural press. He admired the Victorian engineers for their structural developments and the spatial potential these offered, and acknowledged functionalists such as Walter Gropius. However he felt that purely functional solutions did not fulfil human emotional needs and that modern architecture, especially ecclesiastical architecture, needed to take account of the developments – above all spatial developments – made by modern artists. He could see value in Le Corbusier's works, yet criticised his chapel at Ronchamp for the obscurity of its symbolism.

Pace qualified through indenture with experienced architects alongside part-time study at the Regent Street Polytechnic, acquiring practical skills during the day in parallel with a more theoretical education in the evenings. These he supplemented by private study, reading extensively and making detailed observations of buildings, particularly vernacular architecture. The result was a training rooted at once in modernism and the Arts and Crafts style, which endowed him with a commitment to functionalist design alongside a respect for traditional materials and craftsmanship.

Pace was a progressive churchman, championing liturgical reform and the church's adoption of modernism. He was a member of the New Churches Research Group founded in 1957 and before that of an equivalent group in Hull. Two modernising deans – Eric Milner White in York and Glyn Simon at Llandaff – became his principal patrons, and through them he came to intervene in some 500 churches in Yorkshire and more than 80 in South Wales. Milner White's shared interest in craftsmanship and modern art confirmed Pace's decision to establish his office in York, rather than seek the greater publicity possible from a base in London.

Pace's church planning was as innovative as commissions allowed, given that he rarely had the opportunity to build from scratch. In accordance with liturgical renewal he aimed to involve congregations in the rites by removing any separation between them and the sanctuary, bringing the altar forward and clustering them around it. Within a single uninterrupted space he focused attention on the essential elements of altar, font and pulpit, establishing a hierarchy through differences of height and daylighting. Pace exploited modern rolled steel and glulam timbers to make his interiors dramatic. Yet simultaneously he cherished working in traditional materials, albeit in new ways, with limed oak becoming a hallmark. He also reused fittings, in part for economy but also to incorporate memories of their previous situation. His employment of a relatively small number of trusted craftsmen and artists enabled him to delegate some detailing, and hence to undertake such a large number of commissions.

Judi Loach

LEFT St Leonard and St Jude, Doncaster, 1957–63.

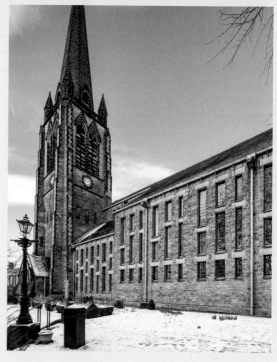

ABOVE, TOP AND ABOVE, LEFT All Saints, Intake, Doncaster, 1951–56.
ABOVE, RIGHT St Mark's, Broomhill, Sheffield, rebuilding of the body of the church incorporating the earlier tower, 1958–63.

ABOVE, TOP St Mark, Chadderton, 1962–63.
ABOVE St Saviour's, Fairweather Green, Bradford, 1964–65, 1971.

Practice Profile:
Gillespie, Kidd & Coia

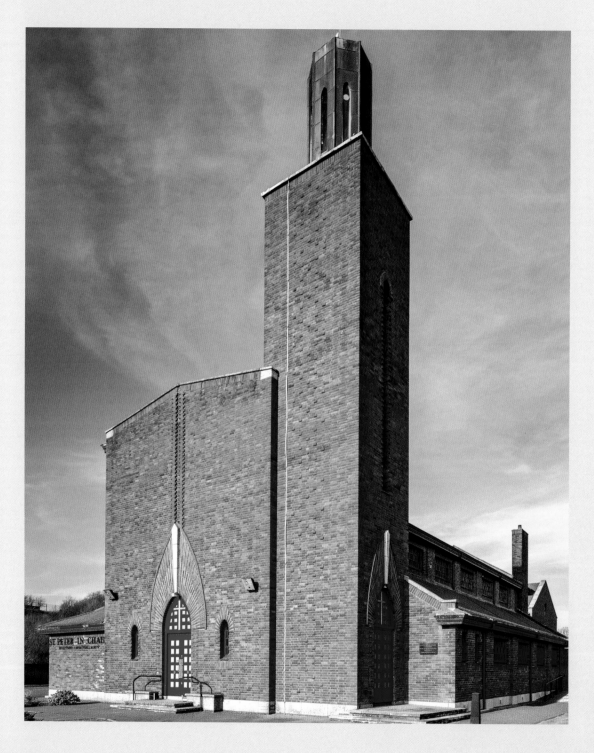

In 1928, the firm's only remaining partner, approached the Roman Catholic Archbishop Mackintosh of Glasgow, who commissioned him for St Anne's, Dennistoun – to which Jack Coia applied his enthusiasm for Renaissance and contemporary Italian church architecture. More churches followed. T. Warnett Kennedy joined in 1933, designing St Peter in Chains, Ardrossan and undoubtedly assisting on St Columba, Hopehill and St Columbkille, Rutherglen. He also designed the Roman Catholic pavilion for the 1938 Empire Exhibition in Glasgow, a curved white modernist building including a chapel and exhibition of ecclesiastical art.

Isi Metzstein arrived in 1945 when, despite post-war austerity, there were numerous churches on the go, the best St Laurence, Greenock, continuing the expressionist theme with pointed parabolic arches in concrete. An improving economy gave greater scope: St Kessog, Balloch, had a pleasing Festival of Britain quality, and St Michael, Dumbarton echoes churches by Fritz Metzger translated into red brick. The firm rapidly moved into more brutalist paths after Andy MacMillan was poached from East Kilbride Development Corporation. Holy Family, Port Glasgow, and St Paul, Shettleston, are often overlooked, as is St Charles, Kelvinside, a Catholic reinterpretation of Coventry Cathedral with folded concrete vaults and brick planes tempered with lashings of marble.

GKC collaborated with many artists. Archibald Dawson contributed sculpture in the 1930s, Benno Schotz did figurative sculpture, notably at Kelvinside and Glenrothes. William Crosbie, who had worked with Fernand Léger in Paris, featured at Rutherglen and Greenock. Later churches used fewer artworks, but Sacred Heart, Cumbernauld, included *dalle de verre* by Sadie McLellan. Only with St Paul, Glenrothes, did the firm reach wider renown. St Bride, East Kilbride, eschewed modesty for monumentality.

Le Corbusier and Aalto were now profound influences in churches that were as scholarly as they were creative – including St Patrick, Kilsyth; St Martin, Castlemilk and Our Lady of the Angels, Falkirk. The seminary, St Peter's, Cardross, occupied the firm for over a decade, a brutalist complex somewhere between La Tourette and the Barbican. Liturgical ideas appeared slowly: St Joseph, Duntocher, was the first with a centralised plan, an idea pursued at Sacred Heart, Cumbernauld; St Benedict, Drumchapel and St Margaret, Clydebank, a space-frame roof bristling over a broad curved plan. They also built a small Lutheran church at East Kilbride and Robinson College, Cambridge, included a chapel. Constantly diverse and inventive, the firm's church architecture reflects and amplifies Roman Catholic self-confidence in 20th-century Scotland, as the architects' modernist obsessions satisfied the clergy's desire to project a contemporary image.

Robert Proctor

LEFT St Peter in Chains, Ardrossan, 1938.

ABOVE , TOP St Patrick, Kilsyth, Lanarkshire, 1961–65.
ABOVE St Paul, Glenrothes, Fife, 1956–57.

ABOVE TOP-LEFT St Paul, Glenrothes, west screen. **ABOVE TOP-RIGHT** St Bride, East Kilbride (1963–64, campanile demolished 1983) **ABOVE** Robinson College Chapel, Cambridge, 1974–80.

Practice Profile:
Maguire & Murray

Liturgical Reform was led by the New Churches Research Group. The priest and polymath Peter Hammond had heard of Bob Maguire's commission for St Paul's Bow Common and got in touch with him and Keith Murray: the group was born. Liturgical reform meant paying close attention to the way the service was conducted, the movements of the congregants and clergy, and fashioning the spaces accordingly. It was a kind of functionalism, a questioning almost from first principles of what a church should be.

Maguire & Murray churches were centralised forms, somewhat similar to corresponding advances in theatre design, using space and materials to highlight the most crucial aspects of the liturgy. St Paul, Bow Common and St Matthew, Perry Beeches are exemplary; other examples followed, each one subtly differentiated by dint of location and type of congregation, together with numerous re-orderings that breathed new life into old churches such as at Abingdon and Thame. The Abbey Church at West Malling, Kent, is a sophisticated insertion of new fabric into a historic setting, and deals sensitively with the required privacy of the nuns. They embraced new technology, notably at St Joseph the Worker, Northolt, where the white-painted steel structure braces the zinc-clad box of the sanctuary in an aesthetic worthy of the early High Tech designers.

If Bob Maguire brought an incisive, architectural mind to their partnership, Keith Murray contributed a craftsman's sensibility. Prior to going into partnership with Maguire in 1959, he had been at the helm of the country's leading ecclesiastical outfitter's and had designed silverware and vestments. Like Hammond, he had travelled in Asia Minor and the Balkans, and had developed a keen interest in Eastern Orthodoxy. 'Things' mattered to Murray, and the practice's churches are well-judged intellectual constructs and included well-crafted (but rarely expensive) objects. In a joint lecture given in 1961 they pondered that phrase from the Lord's Prayer, 'Give us this day our daily bread' and asked themselves why a loaf of supermarket sliced bread wouldn't do: 'It is simply because it has a symbolic content... not expressive of... deep-rooted meanings'. Maguire & Murray felt much affinity with the anti-positivist philosophies of Ernst Cassirer's 'symbolic forms' and were sympathetic to his pupil Susanne Langer's *Feeling and Form* (1953). Sit in a pew in one of their churches, or walk from entrance to font, to altar, and you are bound to sense that '[a] place... is a created thing, an ethnic domain made visible, tangible, sensible'. The partnership's churches are each imbued with a well-judged sense of place, but are alive to the era in which they were built. They testify to the very best contributions architecture had to make in a sometimes bleak post-war Britain: these are buildings of head, hand and heart.

Gerald Adler

LEFT St Joseph the Worker, Northolt, Ealing, 1965–70.

ABOVE, TOP St Joseph the Worker, Northolt, Ealing, 1965–70.
ABOVE Abbey Church, West Malling, Kent, 1962–66.

ABOVE, TOP St Paul, Bow Common, London, 1958–60.
ABOVE St Matthew, Perry Beeches, Birmingham, 1959–63.

GLOSSARY

Altar: The term first used by early Christians to describe the table used for the first Eucharist, the taking of bread and wine to symbolise Christ's body and blood. Stone was used from the 16th century in Britain, and from the 13th century altars were placed at the east end, separated from the congregation.

Ambone: An elevated platform for the reading of scriptures or the litanies (also called an ambo).

Anglo Catholics: Members of the Church of England whose form of worship emphasises its Catholic heritage, at its height in the years 1900–40.

Apse: A rounded end to a chancel.

Arcade: Lines of arches, usually separating a nave and aisles.

Art Sacré: The French artistic movement that sought to create church art of the highest quality, using first-rate (often abstract) artists even if they were non-believers.

Baldachin or baldacchino: A canopy suspended over the altar, more properly a ciborium (q.v.).

Basilica: An early form of church, with a long nave, with aisles, lit by a clerestory and with an apsidal east end.

Benedictines: The rule of St Benedict of Nursia c.480–c.550 provided a code that was a model for all subsequent forms of monasticism in Western Europe, without itself ever becoming a formal order.

Catafalque: A platform to support a coffin, or a structure used at a requiem Mass to represent the body in its absence.

Catenary arch: An elliptical arch taking the natural form adopted by a chain and considered particularly strong.

Chancel: The part of the church, traditionally at the east end, reserved for the choir and celebrants, and containing the sanctuary (q.v.)

Church of England: The English branch of the Western or Latin church which, since Henry VIII rejected the Pope's authority in 1534, has had the sovereign as its head. Within the church are many practices, with 'High' churches or Anglo-Catholics adopting the vestments, rituals and incense of Roman rites, and 'Low' churches concentrating on scriptures and testimony.

Ciborium: A large canopy or test of wood, stone or metal above an altar, carried on columns.

Clerestory: A line of high windows, most common in the nave of the church, traditionally filled with clear glass.

Congregational Church: A non-conformist sect founded by Robert Browne (c.1550–c.1633) in 1592. It expanded in the 19th century, but had declined by 1972 when most of it merged with the English Presbyterians to form the United Reformed Church.

Cosmati work: Marble panels inlaid with mosaic, stones and gilding.

Dalle de verre: A technique of setting thick, chipped and/or faceted 'stones' of glass into concrete or resin.

Decorated Gothic style: the increasingly elaborate Gothic architecture of 1250–1350.

Diagrid: A structure formed of diagonal beams, usually of concrete, allowing broad spans and giving a semblance of vaulting to a church.

English Altar: A carefully prescribed form of altar, usually with curtains or riddells supported on posts, first developed in the 1890s.

Fléche: A small spire or spirelet of wood at the centre of a roof.

Font: In most churches a small basin within a stand used for holding water to sprinkle on an infant in baptism; a few non-conformist churches have revived the full adult immersion adopted by the first Christians and consequently have a tank at the front of their sanctuaries.

Greek cross plan: A church with a central space flanked by four arms of equal length.

Hypberbolic paraboloid roof: A thin concrete, or occasionally timber, roof formed of convex and/ or concave shapes which give it great strength. In a 'hypar', every point on its surface lies on two straight lines, making shuttering relatively easy to construct.

Lady chapel: A chapel ancillary to the main space dedicated to the Virgin Mary, mother of Christ.

Lutheran church: A Protestant or reformed church established by Martin Luther (1483–1546), an Augustinian monk whose studies brought him to believe that scripture was the sole rule of faith, and to challenge the (then often corrupt) hierarchy of the Roman Catholic Church.

Nave: (from the Latin 'navis', meaning ship). The body of the church, traditionally taking the form of a hall at its western end perhaps with lower side sections or aisles separated by arcades (q.v.), where the congregation sits.

Parabolic: (see Hyperbolic paraboloid roof).

Perpendicular Gothic: the stripped down, soaring architecture developed in England from the Black Death (1348–50) to the mid-16th century Reformation.

Pulpit: An elevated platform for a preacher or reader, usually with somewhere to rest books or texts.

Reformation: Schism in western Christianity initiated by Martin Luther in 1517.

Reredos: A decorative stone or timber screen, usually supported on a shelf (predella) covering the wall behind an altar or filling the space between two piers to the east of a sanctuary.

Reservation: The practice of reserving the consecrated bread for Communion in a special receptacle above the altar, such as a tabernacle or (if hanging) a pyx.

Rood loft: A gallery set over a rood screen or chancel screen, perhaps holding figures. In the Middle Ages such a gallery could hold singers or musicians, but in 1561 these were removed to a west gallery and most roods were destroyed. They enjoyed a partial revival in the 19th/ early 20th century.

Roman Catholic Church: That part of the Christian Church which is in communion with the Pope, whose office is directly descended from St Peter and the Apostles in whom Christ invested the power of the Holy Spirit.

Romanesque: Christian architecture of c.1050–1189 defined by relatively small round-arched openings in heavy masonry, semi-circular vaults and apsed east ends.

Sanctuary: The part of the church containing the altar, or – if more than one – the high altar, and a focus for the church's main decoration.

Squinch: An arch or series of concentric arches constructed within the angle between two walls to support a spire or dome.

Tympanum: The space enclosed within a pediment or between a lintel and the arch above, often in an entrance.

Vatican II (Second Vatican Council): The conference on the liturgy held in 1962–65, and used as a shorthand to refer to changes made around that time.

Vierendeel truss: A truss where the members are not triangulated but form rectangular openings in a frame with fixed joints that are capable of transferring and resisting bending moments, developed by Arthur Vierendeel in 1896.

Westwerk/ Westwork: a monumental west end, usually with a tower or towers, most celebrated in western Germany.

FURTHER READING

Gerald Adler, *Robert Maguire & Keith Murray*, London, RIBA Enterprises, 2012

Louise Campbell, *Coventry Cathedral: Art and Architecture in Post-war Britain*, Oxford, Clarendon Press, 1996

Louise Campbell, Miles Glendinning and Jane Thomas, eds., *Basil Spence, Buildings and Projects*, London, RIBA, 2007

Fifty Modern Churches, London, Incorporated Church Building Society, 1947

Mac Journal One: Gillespie, Kidd & Coia, Glasgow, Mackintosh School of Architecture, 1994

Peter Hammond, *Liturgy and Architecture*, London, Barrie and Rockliff, 1960

Elain Harwood, *Space, Hope and Brutalism*, London, Yale University Press, 2015

Elain Harwood and James O. Davies, *England's Post-War Listed Buildings*, London, Batsford, 2015

Christine Hui Lan Manley, *Frederick Gibberd*, Swindon, Historic England, 2017

Christopher Martin, *A Glimpse of Heaven: Catholic churches of England and Wales*, Swindon, English Heritage, 2006

New Churches Illustrated 1926–1936, London, Incorporated Church Building Society, 1936

Peter Pace, *The Architecture of George Pace*, London, Batsford, 1990

Alan Powers, ed., *H.S. Goodhart-Rendel 1887–1959*, London, Architectural Association, 1987

Alan Powers, *Francis Pollen*, Oxford, Robert Dugdale, 1999

Robert Proctor, *Building the Modern Church: Roman Catholic Church Architecture in Britain, 1955 to 1975*, Farnham, Ashgate, 2014

Kenneth Richardson, *The 'Twenty-Five' Churches of the Southwark Diocese, An Inter-war Campaign of Church-building*, London, Ecclesiological Society, 2002

Johnny Rodger, *Gillespie, Kidd & Coia: Architecture 1956–1987*, Edinburgh, RIAS, 2007

Sixty Post-War Churches, London, Incorporated Church Building Society, 1956

G. E. Kidder Smith, *The New Churches of Europe*, London, Architectural Press, 1963

Anthony Symondson, *Stephen Dykes Bower*, London, RIBA, 2011

Anthony Symondson and Stephen Bucknall, *Sir Ninian Comper*, Reading, Spire Books, 2006

Twentieth Century Architecture, no.3, *The Twentieth Century Church*, London, C20 Society, 1998

Christopher Wakeling, *Chapels of England: Buildings of Protestant Nonconformity*, London, Historic England, 2017

Michael Yelton and John Salmon, *Anglican Church-Building in London 1915–1945*, Reading, Spire Books, 2007

Michael Yelton and John Salmon, *Anglican Church-Building in London 1946–2012*, Reading, Spire Books, 2013

INTRODUCTION

It was a 75-degree winter day in San Diego. The warm Santa Ana winds were blowing lazily off the desert and out to sea. Palm trees rustled their skirts like swaying fan dancers beneath a cloudless blue sky. On the horizon the Coronado Islands were clearly visible in the dry air after hiding for weeks behind ocean haze. Downtown new mirrored towers glittered amidst the tile roofs and arches of San Diego's older Mission Revival buildings and the world's largest fleet of tuna boats set up a sort of waterfront fence of bristling masts.

High atop Point Loma, at the Cabrillo National Monument—site of the Portuguese navigator Juan Rodríguez Cabrillo's first contact with San Diego Bay in 1542, a man in a San Diego Padres baseball cap swept his binoculars across the scene, picking out landmarks 30 miles away.

'This is why I live in San Diego,' he said, turning to his companions. 'It was so nice this morning that I wanted to do a little of everything—run on the beach, picnic beside El Prado in Balboa Park, take a sailboat out on Mission Bay, or just stay home and garden. Life's tough in Paradise, isn't it?'

Whether it's admiring a stunning day, revelling in a sunset, or becoming indignant when a morning layer of fog hangs near the coast too long, such reactions are all part of life in San Diego. This weather-watching is equivalent in a San Diegan to a Midwestern farmer talking about rainfalls and freezes. Weather dominates the region by its near-perfection. It has always impressed and attracted visitors, from the first wanderers—the San Dieguito Indians— around 10,000 BC, to a doctor in the late 1800s who went so far as to say that 'The inhabitants have secured a large stock of thermometers and pulviometers and have zealous meteorologists, and are determined to demonstrate the unparalleled sanitary values of their growing burgh.' His spiel worked—thousands came to San Diego solely to improve their health.

Photographers, also, have been impressed. There is nothing quite like San Diego light, be it slanting across the Laguna Mountains, a high range that separates San Diego from the desert, or dropping its salmon-colored curtains into the West's unbroken horizon. Photographers find images at every turn.

San Diego is a large city that covers about 300 square miles and in population it is now the eighth metropolis in the United States. Spurts of growth have gripped the area several times since Franciscan Father Junipero Serra founded Mission San Diego de Alcalá in 1769—so laying the anchor of the California mission chain. Early explorers could see at once that the land surrounding the harbor Cabrillo had discovered was perfect for settlement. It consisted of low and fairly flat mesas, cut by perennial streams running to the sea. One great valley unfolded eastward from the bay, following the course of the San Diego River. It would host the first serious settlements in the area under the typical Spanish three-part plan of colonization in the New World—establish a mission, a presidio, and a pueblo, and don't forget to look for gold.

Throughout the Spanish and Mexican eras of development, San Diego's residents clustered around the garrison on a hillside above the San Diego River. Eventually a town grew up around a small dusty plaza (literally jumping with fleas), while out near Point Loma the smell led to cowhide houses that traded with ships out of Boston. Much of San Diego's growth was coming from an influx of foreigners (even mountain man Jedediah Smith came through in 1826). They mixed, not always comfortably, with the governing *Mexicanos*.

War between the United States and Mexico in 1846 signalled the end of Mexican rule in San Diego and emphasis soon shifted to Yankee settlement of what was called New Town several miles to the south (the site of today's downtown). A central figure in the boom of

1868 was Alonzo Horton, who parcelled up almost 1,000 acres in and near downtown and saw 226 blocks sell off in a matter of months. Old Town was all but forgotten, with many of its adobe structures crumbling to earthen mounds. Some of the houses remain today though, as part of Old Town State Historic Park, including the restored Casa de Estudillo, one of California's finest courtyard homes from the Mexican period.

Despite the efforts of developer-genius Horton and others after him, San Diego remained just a little further down the railroad line than Los Angeles and always a few steps behind its northern neighbor in growth and commerce (blessedly so, for San Diego has avoided, up to now, much of the sprawl and congestion plaguing Los Angeles). After World War II, growth accelerated again as many veterans who'd shipped out for Pacific duty from San Diego returned to Southern California. The military, especially the US Navy, strengthened its 11th Fleet operations out of San Diego to the point where this became a 'navy town', and it was assumed that a San Diegan must be connected to the military in some way—at least through someone in the family.

Life was good up on the mesas. Row upon row of small houses lined the canyon rims, many with eclectic little gardens growing everything from banana plants and cactus to limes and lemons. The beaches, having started with the first heyday of tent cities in Coronado, continued to be a summer-long attraction and cottages shouldered their way into the sandy strip that separated the surf from Mission Bay. Tourism came into its own when Mission Bay was dredged to create a huge playland for small boats bordered by parks and hotels. The city's growth was shifting almost imperceptibly to the north and once again Mission Valley, only steps from the first houses of the *padres*, was the focus. Downtown languished, its major retail stores drawn to the new shopping centers in the valley, its office buildings squat and dreary.

Today, 20 years after the retail exodus began, downtown is back in favor again. Millions of square feet of office space are opening up in bold new towers, and a downtown shopping center named for Horton is the key to center-city redevelopment. After years of not having an outdoor restaurant or sidewalk café, downtown is aswirl

with pedestrians munching hotdogs at vendors' carts, sipping espresso at small tables beneath tassled umbrellas and strolling the waterfront promenades of Seaport Village—a Disneyesque collection of shops and restaurants on San Diego Harbor. Where you once would have expected to find a smelly cannery, the new Hotel Intercontinental's gleaming ellipse rises like a sail above the shipyards.

The Gaslamp Quarter, all that remains of Horton's New Town, is struggling back from being skid row to become a historic district with newly bricked sidewalks, offices, shops, and restaurants. Artists have moved into lofts wherever they can find them south of Market, often putting up with the hum of sewing machines from garment factories above and below, while more than a dozen art galleries have opened in the last two years.

The city is *alive* again, thank you, and unlike most urban centers it keeps a small-town feeling, amidst the steel and glass, so that it's usual for an office worker to run into an acquaintance at lunch and to greet shopowners and waiters by name. Old haunts are being replaced by new, just as steak sandwiches gave way recently to pasta, salads and sushi.

Through it all runs an almost invisible thread that ties the city, after 225 years, to Mexico. At times the whole relationship twists into a Gordian knot. The Mexico–US border area is one of San Diego's greatest tourist assets, yet it is plagued by illegal immigration and a lack of fundamental city services, such as adequate sewage treatment, on the Mexico side. Tijuana (no, it is not called Ti-*a*-wana) is a vibrant city full of colors never seen on buildings north of the border, *mercados* bursting with tropical fruits, citrus, birds in bamboo cages, *piñatas*, and beggar children selling Chiclets. *Panaderias* (bakeries) fill the air with the aroma of fresh-baked *bolillos* (crusty rolls), and wonderful restaurants serve a cuisine quite unlike the 'Mexican' food (the too-familiar ground-beef tacos, beans, and rice) found north of the border. The 'Line' is like a cultural tidal zone surging daily with commerce and tourism, mixing poverty with prosperity. Typical of the dichotomy is the news that recently, with little fanfare, Tijuana's millions passed San Diego in population size—yet over half the city's houses do not have running water.

The tourists' San Diego is richer than ever. At the Zoo, new animal habitats include an open primate area where visitors walk on aerial platforms to stand at eye level with chimps in the treetops. In Wild Animal Park, a zoo without cages, the birth rate among free-roaming animals is astoundingly high. Sea World's new Penguin Encounter, a frigid aquarium for serious ornithological study, is every bit as popular as their circus-like whale and dolphin shows. Balboa Park, originally set aside by city planners in 1868 while Horton's tract was selling off, is a mature park of grand buildings strung out along El Prado; a promenade built for the Panama–California Exposition, 1915-16. Behind the richly decorated facades are museums and exhibit halls, and you have a wide choice from anthropology to Cézanne, from model train exhibits to the photography of Diane Arbus.

Above all, this is a water city where you can skin-dive, deep-sea fish, surf, waterski, skipper a Hobie Cat, windsurf, jetski, waterski, canoe, crew. Pick any imaginable water sport, and it's bound to be a year-round activity on San Diego's saltwater (and on dozens of inland reservoirs). This is a city of fitness buffs, and the sport of triathlon (where contestants swim in the ocean, bike-ride, and run over marathon distances consecutively) started when an athletic club on Mission Bay dreamed up the 'Ironman' concept. San Diegans *know* how to play.

San Diegans' favorite Sunday drive (or bicycle ride) is along the coast highway northward from Pacific Beach. La Jolla, the 'jewel' of golden cliffs laced with caves, has grown from a few cottages and hotels above the coves to become San Diego's most prestigious address—both for homes and office buildings. Whatever the changing nature of the town, out in the water, floating a few feet above the submerged, grass-bearded reefs, snorkelers find peace—and hope for a glimpse of bright orange garibaldi fish.

Interstate highways crisscross the city and county and are comparatively free of the bumper-to-bumper coagulation that seizes up other cities. In one extraordinary stretch near downtown, Interstate 5 passes under the flight path for the airport and the incoming jets look as if they're about to leave skid marks on your car's roof. These highways open up San Diego's incredible diversity, from the flower fields of North County, draped like banners across the hillsides, to the old mining town of Julian in the Cuyamaca backcountry. This is a big place and no one can see it in a few days or even a week. Those with orderly prioritized schedules will only cry out in frustration; at every turn there is something to trap you for a day of pleasure rather than just an hour of looking around.

To be sure, there is some trouble in Paradise. Bulldozers graze the canyons like big, geometrically minded sheep, terracing the land into a Mayan look for new housing subdivisions. Dozens of citizen groups go before City Council each year in protest; some of them succeed in having canyons set aside as urban wilderness preserve. S.O.H.O. (Save Our Heritage Organization) and the San Diego Historical Society have been models for the rest of the country, preserving many of San Diego's finest buildings. But they've also lost out often, among their losses being a few works of Irving Gill, the city's internationally known architect of the early 1900s. Downtown you're apt to see a rumpled street-denizen sleeping in a Market Street doorway, as you head for one of the city's lovely little theaters.

You expect these things of any city but somehow in San Diego you suspect they are also avoidable. It wasn't campaign rhetoric that prompted a mayor (now US Senator Pete Wilson) to proclaim San Diego 'America's Finest City'. San Diegans believe it, and they aren't about to be caught 'just passing through'. Sometimes a certain neurosis sets in, prompting bumper stickers such as 'Welcome to San Diego! Now go home.' But for the most part it is pride, not smugness, that powers this city's personality.

It's something simpler, also, than the politics and economics of urban life. It may be the feel of sand shifting between your toes on Torrey Pines beach. It may be breakfasting on your patio in December, or stopping at a strawberry stand in March. You might swim out past the surfline at sunset to be closer to the pelicans doing their crumpled-wing dives for dinner. This place called San Diego is, in the end, like sable against skin—natural!, warm, and very, very comforting.

San Diego, March 1984   PETER JENSEN

1 San Diego Bay, sunrise

Small boats cluster around the margins of Shelter Island—actually a peninsula of parks, marinas, and hotels. Twin hangers at the Coronado Naval Air Station catch the dawn's first rays, while downtown still rests in shadow.

2 *(left)* Coronado's Silver Strand

Condominiums line a narrow isthmus just south of Coronado's grand Hotel 'Del', more properly the Hotel del Coronado, built in 1888. The hotel's peaked-roof boathouse, now restored as a restaurant, sits like a little wedding cake amidst the Coronado Yacht Club sailboats.

3 Bell Tower, Mission San Diego de Alcalá

Father Serra founded the first of California's Franciscan missions on Presidio Hill, San Diego, in 1769 and five years later the mission moved to the present site. Since then fire, earthquake, and in the last century generations of neglect required several reconstructions of this graceful, white-washed church with its five-bell tower. The name of the mission was given in honour of Saint Didacus of Alcalá in Spain. Indirectly this is the original of the city's name also—indirectly only because the site of the future city was named in 1602 by Sebastian Vizcaíno after his flagship, which he had already named after the Spanish saint.

Here aloes lift up their 'red hot pokers' in January outside the mission walls.

4 *(left)* Tuna fleet at anchor, San Diego Bay

A forest of cables, rope ladders, masts and trees stands silhouetted against the sunset along Harbor Drive. A mixed grove of palm trees and seafaring technology. Most of the city's palms were planted in the first decades after 1900, when a sort of botanical fever, led by Kate Sessions, gripped the city. Sophisticated electronic gear still hasn't replaced the classic crow's nests used to spot feeding schools of fish.

5 Sunset from Quail Botanical Gardens

Multitrunk eucalyptus trees cage the horizon high on a hill in Encinitas, where a small botanical garden abounds with exotic plants.

6 *(left)* La Jolla Cove

Pockets of sand collect along La Jolla's rocky coast. The protected cove is a favorite with snorkelers who flipper out a few dozen yards to grassy reefs.

7 The *Star of India*, Maritime Museum

Sails set, but anchored forever along the Embarcadero, the *Star of India* is the oldest steel-hulled sailing ship afloat. Behind her is the ferryboat *Berkeley* and the steam yacht *Media*, all part of the Maritime Museum.

8 Downtown San Diego from Shelter Island

Viewed from atop the Sheraton Harbor Island Hotel, downtown's towers
are still ablaze with lights just after sunset. A riverboat turned restaurant
is just distinguishable at the causeway's end.

9 Seaport Village

A waterfront development within walking distance of downtown, Seaport Village is an amalgam of New England, Western, and Mediterranean-style architecture, housing shops and restaurants.

10 Point Loma cliffs, high tide

Geologic strata have been stripped back by waves at the entrance to San Diego Bay. Tidepoolers can venture 100 yards or more from the base of the cliffs at low tide.

11 *(right)* Community Concourse in downtown San Diego

Downtown's Community Concourse (built in the mid-1960s) is a mix of city offices, Civic Theater (shown here), sculpture and fountain, and a convention center. At noon, the plaza is a gathering place for office workers basking in the sun.

12 *(left)* Point Loma and the entrance to San Diego Bay

Juan Rodríguez Cabrillo rounded these rugged scarps on 28 September 1542 and sailed into a calm, estuarine bay. Today the Point is one of America's most popular National Monuments in terms of visitor numbers (the main attraction is the spectacular view). The old lighthouse, a lone white building, can be seen at the Point's summit.

13 Hotel Del Coronado

San Diego's great Victorian lady, the Hotel 'Del', has been a symbol of tourist luxury since it was built in 1888 and is the last surviving Victorian resort of its kind in California. The octagonal roof-crown, a masterpiece of wooden construction, shelters several ballrooms and restaurants.

14 Mission San Luis Rey de Francia, east of Oceanside

A day's horseback ride north of Mission San Diego de Alcalá and midway between San Diego and San Juan Capistrano, this 'the King of the Missions' was founded in 1789 and named after Louis XI of France. It was the largest of the missions, with a church that could hold a thousand people.

15 *(right)* Heritage Park

These houses were moved here by conservationists from around the city as the wrecker's ball threatened and in this way a new neighborhood was created on a hill above Old Town State Historic Park.

16 Tortilla making in Old Town

Masa, corn softened in limewater and then stone ground, is patted by hand to make the traditional Mexican *tortilla*. Demonstration at Bazaar del Mundo in Old Town takes place on weekends.

17 Posada ceremony, Mission San Luis Rey

The holy family's journey to Bethlehem is recreated at parish churches each Christmastide in San Diego's Latin communities. Both of the missions in San Diego County still serve congregations.

18 *(left)* Tuna boats on the Embarcadero

Twin empty tuna seiners, floating high in the water, await their first trip. The tuna industry, severely depressed in the 1980s, is beset by boundary disputes in foreign waters as captains range their boats further and further from San Diego, often following warm-water currents down the coast of South America.

19 Spiral stairway, Point Loma lighthouse

Like the inside of a chambered shell, tower stairs invite National Monument visitors up to look at the lighthouse's beveled Fresnel lens.

20 Sculpture, high-tech office complex

Stargazer by Alexander Lieberman shoots skyward from the grounds of the San Diego Tech Center, one of many new research and development office parks in the Sorrento Valley area, north of downtown San Diego.

21 *(right)* San Diego Trolley

Linking downtown with the San Ysidro–Tijuana border crossing since 1982, the bright-red 'trolley' (actually a state-of-the-art German-made electric train) is a new lightrail transit system laid out over old railroad rights of way.

22 *(left)* Chart House Restaurant, Coronado
One of the city's most picturesque buildings was once the Hotel 'Del' boathouse. Yachters can anchor nearby and row over for famous steak-and-lobster dinners.

23 Broadway and the financial district
Strings of stoplights flash on San Diego's major downtown thoroughfare. City blocks are small, and most of the streets narrow.

24 Armed Forces Day, Broadway Pier

On weekends, a Navy ship usually ties up to the Broadway Pier and opens to the public. Armed Forces Day brings the added spectacle of Navy bands and color reviews.

25 *(right)* U.C.S.D. Library

The late San Diego architectural critic James Britton described this library, designed by the William Pereira group, as 'hovering for all the world like an intelligence-stocked spaceship from a better planet.'

26 Neon reflections, Gaslamp Quarter

Gaslamp theatre marquees create a gaudy display of color along Fifth Avenue in what is for the most part a district of historic buildings.

27 *(right)* Pacific Beach

Scallops of retreating waves etch a beach widened by summer's deposits of sand. In winter, much of the coastline is stripped down to its rock-bed by storm waves.

28 *(left)* Ranunculus fields, Encinitas

The cool coastal climate zone in Encinitas on the county's north coast is ideal for growing flowers—for cuttings, nursery stock, and seed. Here a tour group discovers why Encinitas is called by local promoters 'The Flower Capital of the World'.

29 La Jolla and Children's Pool Beach

The curving seawall was built at the turn of the century to create a safe, shallow, wading pool for children. Today this is mostly dry beach, but is still a favorite haven for families with toddlers. The bulky condominium tower helped precipitate laws limiting highrise buildings so close to the coast.

30 Wild Animal Park, San Pasqual Valley

San Diego Wild Animal Park near Escondido is an extension of the San Diego Zoo—with a big difference; animals roam across a huge, almost indiscernibly fenced area of hillsides and plains. Visitors tour from veldt to rain forest on a monorail. In the main compound area, primates clamber up eucalyptus trunks next to a restaurant patio, manmade lakes, and amphitheaters featuring trained animal shows.

31 Ocotillo plant, Anza-Borrego

Twisted limbs of ocotillo will turn a bright orange in spring with thousands of tiny petalled flowers set amidst the spikes.

32 *(left)* Harbor Island Marina
San Diego Bay's marshy edges were dredged to create a huge small-boat marina. The city is called home by some of the world's best sailors, including America's Cup captain Dennis Connor.

33 La Jolla shoreline
Layered rocks, an Upper Cretaceous formation typical of the shoreline from Point Loma to La Jolla, are part of the coastal terrace laid bare by the waves.

46 Sunset cliffs

Magnificent walls of sedimentary rock between Point Loma and Ocean Beach, seen here in the golden light of late afternoon.

47 *(right)* Tuna nets, Embarcadero

Mountainous piles of nets await repair and reloading on the docks along Harbor Drive. Nets have been modified in recent years to reduce the number of porpoises entangled and drowned in the fishing haul.

48 Scripps Pier

The world-renowned oceanographic research center's pier stretches out past the surfline to service some of the University of California's vessels. In the background, residential areas of La Jolla.

49 *(right)* Dolphin show, Sea World

Underwater signals send dolphins through their acrobatic maneuvers at one of Sea World's many saltwater pools that are fed by the waters of Mission Bay.

50 Silver Strand condominiums

Seen from the ocean side, highrise residences bask in the afternoon sun; visitors scramble on the rock breakwater in front of the Hotel Del Coronado. The Coronado peninsula is also the site of a navy training school, so that a beach adjacent to the southernmost luxury tower is the training ground for the élite Naval underwater demolition teams.

51 San Diego Museum of Art

Most ornate of the buildings constructed for the 1915–16 Panama-
California Exposition, the Museum of Man's facade is reminiscent of
Mexico's great cathedrals. Inside is an extensive collection of American
Indian artefacts. Shows range from shamanism to Halloween hauntings.

52 Badland Caves, Anza-Borrego

The desert is a place of discovery and surprise. Here, in a land of little water, caves cut by sudden rainfalls and flashflooding over thousands of years wend their way beneath the Badland Hills.

53 *(right)* Aerial view of Torrey Pines Cliffs

Table Rock juts from the shoreline beneath the state reserve; clearly it is almost an island. This formation is sometimes called Bathtub Rock, on account of a mysterious tub-sized depression filled with tidewater—dug out, some say, by a crazy coal miner.

54 Chicano Park, Barrio Logan

Concrete ramps to the Coronado Bridge became 'canvases' for local Chicano artists after the freeways cut through their neighborhood. Now the murals are the pride of the *barrio*.

55 Horton Plaza fountain
Three-quarters of a century old and still flowing, the fountain is the historic center of downtown. The Plaza area is now the site of a massive redevelopment project involving a multiblock shopping center, theaters and hotels.

56 California Tower, Balboa Park

A New York architect, Bertram Grosvenor Goodhue, brought his magic to the Panama-California Exposition of 1915–16 and San Diego has never looked the same since. Goodhue himself planned that most of the buildings with their temporary false fronts would be torn down to make way for gardens, but the structures, including this landmark tower, proved too endearing to San Diegans.

57 *(right)* Serra Museum, Presidio Park above Old Town

Often mistaken by tourists for Mission San Diego de Alcalá, Serra Museum crowns a hill near the intersection of Interstates 8 and 5 and is home to the San Diego Historical Society. Nearby is the site of the original Spanish presidio.

58 Anza-Borrego looking toward Mount Laguna

The nation's largest state park presents geology on a monumental scale—fault zones, granitic rocks of the Southern California batholith, and flash-flood washes.

59 *(right)* Tuna seiner off Point Loma

As a squall line approaches, a lone tuna seiner heads for harbor around Point Loma. The boats have a distinctive silhouette—high bow and low stern.

60 Palm Canyon, Anza-Borrego

Despite summertime temperatures on the valley floor over 110 degrees, Palm Canyon's creek flows year-round (except in severe drought). An hour's walk from park headquarters, native fan-palms clump at the water's edge. Their trunks were once blackened by fire but now the grove is carefully protected.

61 Vacation Village, Mission Bay

A hotel complex of lakes, pools, and bungalows occupies one of Mission Bay's islands. Guests can waterski or sail only steps away from their rooms.

62 *(left)* Mission Beach

High density, high rent. Life shoulder-to-shoulder in the beach communities is thought of as an advantage by many of 'M.B.'s' free spirits. Every house is within two blocks of beach or bay, and some of the city's most outlandish architecture punctuates the sandy boardwalks.

63 'Wall-to-wall' pleasure boats fill the marina at Harbor Island.

64 *(left)* Downtown reflections

The Crocker Bank Building, as seen reflected in a neighboring tower on Broadway.

65 Tiled Dome, Santa Fe Depot

Reminiscent in its style of the mission heritage, downtown's depot is on the National Register of Historic Places. Recent restoration has the old tile gleaming again, especially when seen against the backdrop of a glass curtain wall. The building's outdoor waiting room is gone, but the remainder is still very much unchanged.

66 *(left)* Interstate Highway 5 at sunset

Flowing bands of light against a typically pink sunset sky, Interstate 5 and the First Street bridge mark the northwest edge of downtown. The freeway at this point swings east, then south towards the border in a tight S-curve around the city's heart.

67 Fat City Restaurant, Pacific Coast Highway

Restauranteur Tom Fat, descendant of Chinese laborers who came to California during the 1849 Gold Rush, turned San Diego on its ear with his neon interpretation of an Art Deco theme. Fat City serves continental cuisine, while a companion restaurant in the same building, China Camp, offers 'California-Chinese' fare.

68 Old Globe Theatre, Balboa Park

Home of the San Diego Shakespeare Festival, the Old Globe was rebuilt
after a tragic fire. The house is rarely without a performance and brings a
wide range of drama to San Diego theatregoers.

69 Suburban development, La Jolla area

As San Diego's growth spreads in three directions (only the ocean can stop
the inevitable and then only on one side), new neighborhoods of single
and multifamily homes line the graded hills. The city has adopted a
controlled growth plan through the end of the century.

70 *(left)* La Jolla Headlands

While waves pound these La Jolla cliffs, bathers can swim in a quiet cove just around the point. Red-roofed buildings in the distance across La Jolla Bay mark the La Jolla Beach and Tennis Club.

71 Palm Canyon waterfall

Hikers climb from one boulder-rimmed pool to another high above Anza-Borrego's main campground. Watering holes support a small herd of rare bighorn sheep.

72 Tuna nets, San Diego Bay

Tugged into the air by the seiners' powerful winches, nets are draped onto the stern decks as crewmen check for damage.

73 *(right)* Sculpture, United States Court-house

Artist Beverly Pepper's *Excalibur* spears the plaza across from the Wells Fargo Building. The low railing, a later addition by the city to discourage climbers, is still decried by art critics who loved the sculpture's uninterrupted joining of steel and concrete.

74 Koala bear, San Diego Zoo

No diet problem here; the koala's favorite food, eucalyptus leaves, is abundant in San Diego. The zoo may be best-known for its innovative natural habitats and landscaping—officials estimate the value of its plants as greater than that of its wildlife inhabitants.

75 *(right)* Orangutan, San Diego Zoo

A family of Sumatran orangutans, regal in their flowing coats, occupies one habitat in the zoo's new primate area.

76 *(left)* Navy ship at anchor, San Diego Bay
Home of the 11th Fleet, San Diego sees every
class of naval vessel. At sunset, the gray hull
of this ship shines like burnished copper; its
helicopter sits in shadow on an aft platform.

77 Bodysurfer, Del Mar
Waiting for the next onrush of waves, a lone
bodysurfer tries for just one more ride in the
70-degree summer water.

78 *(left)* Point Loma Lighthouse

The original lighthouse, built of brick rubble in 1855, was later found to be too high up in the fog banks and was replaced by a new light at the surf's edge.

79 Hanglider, Torrey Pines Cliffs

Banking on a wave of wind coming up the cliffs, this hanglider will soar back and forth parallel to the waves far below. The Glider Port, near University of California, San Diego, allows spectators a gull's-eye view.

80 Downtown seen from Point Loma

Shelter Island's marina bristles with masts surrounding the San Diego
Yacht Club. The distant skyline is several miles from the harbor mouth.

81 Seaport Village Restaurant
Stalking into the bay on ungainly legs, this Seaport Village seafood restaurant takes diners closer to the source. Catch of the day in San Diego is often swordfish or yellowtail.

82 & 83 *(overleaf)* La Jolla
Viewed from Scenic Drive near the U.C.S.D. campus, the crescent shape of La Jolla Bay sweeps back from Alligator Head and the famous Cove.

84 *(left)* Iceplant banks near Windansea Beach

Lower tides expose small carpets of sand for sunbathers beneath dazzling flowering ice-plant.

85 Epiphyllum 'Juniper'

Growing on tree trunks in the jungle wild, these exotic 'orchid cactuses' have adapted well to San Diego's climate as lathhouse and indoor plants.

86 Coronado shorefishing

One ruined jetty breaks the sandy line of the Hotel Del Coronado's beach;
 a perfect place to cast a line further into the surf—or try an ambitious line
 or two on larger quarry.